Pick strong structure
re. BT

useful to have
something a a ST/brief
model.

much here relevant
to indiv therapy eg
differentiation, replica
processes etc

good for experienced therapist
lk nw idea?
ccs considering licence?
good intro to Complicated complex couples wk
& particular demands

BASIC TEXTS IN COUNSELLING AND PSYCHOTHERAPY

Series Editor: Stephen Frosh

This series introduces readers to the theory and practice of counselling and psychotherapy across a wide range of topic areas. The books will appeal to anyone wishing to use counselling and psychotherapeutic skills and are particularly relevant to workers in health, education, social work and related settings. The books in this series are unusual in being rooted in psychodynamic and systemic ideas, yet being written at an accessible, readable and introductory level. Each text offers theoretical background and guidance for practice, with creative use of clinical examples.

Published

Jenny Altschuler
WORKING WITH CHRONIC ILLNESS

Bill Barnes, Sheila Ernst and Keith Hyde
AN INTRODUCTION TO GROUPWORK

Stephen Briggs
WORKING WITH ADOLESCENTS

Alex Coren
SHORT-TERM PSYCHOTHERAPY

Jim Crawley and Jan Grant
COUPLE THERAPY

Emilia Dowling and Gill Gorell Barnes
WORKING WITH CHILDREN AND PARENTS THROUGH SEPARATION AND DIVORCE

Loretta Franklin
AN INTRODUCTION TO WORKPLACE COUNSELLING

Gill Gorell Barnes
FAMILY THERAPY IN CHANGING TIMES 2nd ed.

Fran Hedges
AN INTRODUCTION TO SYSTEMIC THERAPY WITH INDIVIDUALS

Sally Hodges
COUNSELLING ADULTS WITH LEARNING DISABILITIES

Linda Hopper
COUNSELLING AND PSYCHOTHERAPY WITH CHILDREN AND ADOLESCENTS

Ravi Rana
COUNSELLING STUDENTS

Tricia Scott
INTEGRATIVE PSYCHOTHERAPY IN HEALTH CARE

Geraldine Shipton
WORKING WITH EATING DISORDERS

Laurence Spurling
AN INTRODUCTION TO PSYCHODYNAMIC COUNSELLING

Paul Terry
COUNSELLING THE ELDERLY AND THEIR CARERS

Steven Walker
CULTURALLY COMPETENT THERAPY

Jan Wiener and Mannie Sher
COUNSELLING AND PSYCHOTHERAPY IN PRIMARY HEALTH CARE

Shula Wilson
DISABILITY, COUNSELLING AND PSYCHOTHERAPY

Invitation to authors

The Series Editor welcomes proposals for new books within the Basic Texts in Counselling and Psychotherapy series. These should be sent to Stephen Frosh at the School of Psychology, Birkbeck College, Malet Street, London WCIE 7HX (email s.frosh@bbk.ac.uk).

Basic Texts in Counselling and Psychotherapy
Series Standing Order ISBN 0-333-69330-2
(*outside North America only*)

You can receive future titles in this series as they are published by placing a standing order. Please contact your bookseller or, in the case of difficulty, write to us at the address below with your name and address, the title of the series and the ISBN quoted above.

Customer Services Department, Macmillan Distribution Ltd.
Houndmills, Basingstoke, Hampshire RG21 6XS, England

COUPLE THERAPY

THE SELF IN THE RELATIONSHIP

JIM CRAWLEY AND JAN GRANT

First published 2008 by
PALGRAVE MACMILLAN
Houndmills, Basingstoke, Hampshire RG21 6XS and
175 Fifth Avenue, New York, N.Y. 10010
Companies and representatives throughout the world

PALGRAVE MACMILLAN is the global academic imprint of the Palgrave
Macmillan division of St. Martin's Press, LLC and of Palgrave Macmillan Ltd.
Macmillan® is a registered trademark in the United States, United Kingdom
and other countries. Palgrave is a registered trademark in the European
Union and other countries.

ISBN-13: 978–1–4039–9490–5
ISBN-10: 1–4039–9490–0

This book is printed on paper suitable for recycling and made from fully
managed and sustained forest sources. Logging, pulping and manufacturing
processes are excepted to conform to the environmental regulations of the
country of origin.

A catalogue record for this book is available from the British Library.

A catalog record for this book is available from the Library of Congress.

10   9   8   7   6   5   4   3   2   1
17   16   15   14   13   12   11   10   09   08

Printed in China

To our partners, Shirley and Guy

CONTENTS

Acknowledgements

As is the case for all who write about psychotherapy, we are very conscious of how much we have learnt from our clients — both those couples we have been able to help and those from whom our learning has come about as a result of being unable to progress to a good outcome in the therapy. The clinical illustrations we give are all based on actual cases, although with details modified to protect confidentiality. We also wish to express our gratitude to our students and supervisees, who have taught us much over the years; to Dr Chris Theunissen and Dr Wendy-Lynne Wolman, who provided critical and helpful comments on an earlier draft of some of the chapters; and Ben Mullings, who assisted with the section on research into couple therapy.

INTRODUCTION

There is no one definition as to what constitutes 'marriage' or 'the couple' that is constant across time and across cultures. Any couple relationship, whether in the form of a legal (de jure) marriage or an informal (de facto) marriage, is at its core a social construct. The form that a particular relationship takes, the expectations that are held for it, and the ways in which the partners to the relationship seek to live out their relationship will always be shaped by social, cultural, and religious factors, as well as by the psychological functioning of the two partners involved. In similar vein, the couple therapist inevitably brings their own culture into the therapy, both consciously and unconsciously in their countertransference to the couple and their relationship (Gould, 2007). These realities must be recognized since they are an essential component of the context for therapy aimed at helping couples with difficulties in their relationship.

In recent decades, the form of the couple relationship in Western societies has been profoundly influenced in two ways. First, there has been the development of modern forms of contraception, in particular oral contraception for women, which has to a significant extent broken the nexus between sexual activity and procreation. Second, there has been a steady process of questioning and change in the role and status of women in society. These changes have inevitably impacted on the couple relationship, not least through a much greater importance now being given to the quality of the relationship, both in terms of emotional and sexual satisfaction and in terms of the quality of companionship.

Today, couples typically enter either a formal or de facto marriage at a later date, and postpone having their first child — if they decide to have children at all — for some years after marriage. Parallel to this has been the development of the new phenomenon of the dual-career couple. Other changes in the form and the experience of contemporary couple relationships include the much higher incidence of step-family or blended-family arrangements, a tendency for children to continue

living in their parents' home until a later age than in previous generations (or to leave, but then return for one or more extended periods),
and the gradual acceptance of same-sex couple relationships in the
community. Another emerging but often unrecognized issue in
Western democracies is that people are retiring earlier from the work-
force and living longer, thereby creating a relatively new and often quite
extensive phase in the family life cycle, the post-retirement couple.

Relationship difficulties constitute one of the more common reasons for people to seek therapy, yet as a specialty in its own right,
couple therapy is relatively new. Couple therapy began with the
development of the marriage guidance movement in the early
1900s. It is, however, only in recent decades that couple therapy
has begun finally to emerge as a modality of therapy in its own
right; initially couple therapy was dominated by ideas and principles of practice from individual therapy, particularly psychoanalytic
psychotherapy (Nichols, 1988). The advent of family systems theory
in the 1950s opened up exciting new ways of conceptualizing the
structure and dynamics of the couple relationship, but work with
couples then frequently came to be seen as simply a sub-set of family
therapy. Couple therapy is now at a point where it can be seen not
only to draw upon and to be enriched by both individual therapy
and family therapy, but also to possess a knowledge base of its own.

In this book we seek to set out both a way of thinking about the
couple relationship and a framework for practice for working with
couples. To do that we draw upon a psychodynamic understanding
of the individual and the way their internal psychological world
shapes their participation in an intimate relationship with a partner.
We draw also upon the insights of family systems theory. We view
tension between relatedness and separateness as being an ongoing
and inevitable struggle for all human beings, resulting in a circular
and reflexive process of both seeking and reacting against intimacy
and vulnerability in the couple relationship. This tension is reflected
in the sub-title of the book, *The Self in the Relationship*.

We can best give a sense of the approach to couple therapy that we
describe in this book by introducing a couple whose relationship is in
difficulty.

Robert and Tilda were in their early 50s when they sought help with
their relationship. They had three children, two had left home and
the youngest was in the process of moving out. They were referred by
Tilda's psychiatrist, following her discharge from hospital. Tilda had
become depressed some 3 years previously, and had been prescribed

2

antidepressant medication. The medication helped to some extent, but when she was faced with looking after her terminally ill mother, her depression worsened and she ended up being hospitalized.

One of the issues that emerged whilst Tilda was in hospital was her long-standing unhappiness in her marriage to Robert, to the point where she couldn't see herself remaining with him. Her main complaint was that Robert was totally absorbed in his business and had been for years; he never really communicated with her, and she now realized that for a long time she had been feeling lonely and unappreciated. For his part, Robert was ambivalent about the marriage: he didn't want to separate, but he was also doubtful as to whether things could really improve much. He experienced Tilda as quickly becoming 'over-emotional' if he tried to talk with her; she never approached things logically, would never join with him in solving any problems they might have; he felt hopeless and helpless about being able to communicate with Tilda in a meaningful way.

If asked, Robert and Tilda would doubtless say that their problem was 'poor communication' — but does that adequately explain their relationship difficulty? What lies behind their inability to communicate more effectively? How is the couple therapist to engage in the task of understanding the dynamics of Robert and Tilda's relationship, and then draw upon that understanding to provide direction and focus for subsequent interventions aimed at bringing about changes in their relationship?

Robert and Tilda each have a story about their own developmental journey as an individual.

Robert grew up as the fourth of five siblings. His father was a warm and kindly man, but not a strong presence in the family: Robert recalled his father readily giving in to his mother when there was any conflict. His mother came from a well-to-do but unhappy family, and was a stern woman for whom there were 'no shades of gray'; she used contempt and shame as a weapon to keep control of the five children. When Robert was quite young, his father was convicted of an offence and served a short term of imprisonment: this was never talked about in the family, but a profound sense of shame seemed to be linked to this. Robert recalls that when his mother was angry with him she would often say in a contemptuous way, 'you are just like your father'. When Robert was about 16 his father died; he and his younger sister were left at home with his mother, and he left school and started work so that he could become 'the man of the house'. Eighteen months later his mother was diagnosed with terminal cancer, and died when Robert was 17.

Tilda grew up as the middle of five siblings in a working-class family. Her father was a warm and demonstrative man, kindly, but not involved with his children. Tilda's mother had experienced an unhappy childhood: her parents divorced when she was in her early teens, and she then experiencing herself as not being wanted by either parent. This was compounded by the experience of physical and emotional cruelty from her step-father, and she ran away from home at the age of 16. Tilda had a difficult relationship with her mother, whom she described as always negative, picking fault. As the middle of five siblings, she often felt on her own as the others paired off; this was repeated at school, where her lack of confidence often left her feeling she was on the edge of the group.

Robert and Tilda met when in their teens, and were married by the time they were 20. Both brought into the marriage an 'agenda' for relationships — their own unique constellation of things they longed for and things they feared or dreaded, things they intuitively knew how to do in an intimate relationship, and things they found difficult or impossible. They 'clicked' — each felt a sense of promise from the other that resonated strongly.

For Robert, there was a bravado and a focus on 'doing' that defined his sense of what it meant to be a man, a husband, and a father. Beneath that bravado, there was a vulnerable sense of himself, an insecurity and a longing for acceptance and nurture, that he had no way of expressing — *especially* not to Tilda, the person whose opinion of him mattered to him the most. Tilda lacked confidence, she doubted that anyone would really understand her or be there emotionally for her, and she had taken in some of her mother's negative expectations about being a woman — all of which was compounded by two miscarriages, by an affair that Robert had early in their relationship, and by Robert's preoccupation with his work. Tilda was attracted by Robert's self-confidence, by his assertiveness, whilst Robert was drawn to Tilda's gentleness and diffidence that held out the promise of a closeness, intimacy, and warmth that he longed for. Yet 30 years later, those qualities that had initially attracted them to each other were now the focus of their disappointments and complaints in the relationship.

Robert and Tilda's relationship, the patterns of interaction they developed, and the unconscious, taken-for-granted assumptions they made about themselves and each other were a product of their individual life journeys and of their core sense of themselves as a man and as a woman. All of that must be taken into account if a therapist is to understand why Robert and Tilda found it so difficult to communicate with and support each other, and then be able to use that understanding to enable them to change as individuals and as a couple. Thus couple therapy must, in our view, take into account both the intrapsychic experience and developmental history of each partner, as well as the interpersonal system of their relationship.

Our account of couple therapy falls into two parts: the first four chapters provide an overview of ways of understanding the nature and functioning of the couple relationship, and the remaining four chapters focusing on issues of practice. This structure is deliberate. We take it as axiomatic that a responsible therapist will see their first task as being to make an assessment, with the aim of arriving at an understanding — even if limited and provisional — of the persons and of the relationship presenting for help. This applies whether the focus of the intervention is an individual, a couple or family, a group, or any other entity. To make an assessment, the therapist must have an adequate grounding in theory that will enable them to understand the dynamics of the entity — the individual, the family, the group — that they are working with. We have long been concerned that many therapists trained in work with individuals or families include expertise in work with couples in the repertoire of services they offer, when in actual fact they have at best a limited understanding of the dynamics specific to the couple relationship.

In writing a book such as this, we have inevitably had to make choices and draw boundaries about the material we can cover. Diversity in couple relationships, such as same-sex couples, bisexual partners, blended families and partners who come from diverse cultures, is a very significant area of practice; each topic has its own literature. Instead of covering each of these topics separately, we have chosen to illustrate some of the issues faced, with a few select clinical examples throughout the text. Although it is important to be familiar with some of the literature in the area, it is equally important to be able to work with our own countertransference in understanding and joining with couples who present issues that are very different from our own experience. In terms of literature, we would like to draw attention to Gill Gorrell-Barnes' (2004) work on family therapy at a time of increasing diversity of family form, and to two recent papers by our colleague Jac Brown on couple therapy with same-sex couples (Brown, 2007a,b).

1

THE PSYCHODYNAMICS OF THE COUPLE RELATIONSHIP: OBJECT RELATIONS THEORY

Each individual brings unique expectations, wishes, fantasies, conflicts, and style of relating to a couple relationship. Some of this material is conscious and amenable to therapeutic interventions that develop the partners' skills in listening, negotiation, compromise, and 'fighting fair'. However, much of that which drives repetitive couple conflict lies within the unconscious realm, is laden with strong affect, originates in early relationships, and is much less amenable to these conscious attempts to positively restructure interactions (Donovan, 2003). We believe that the couple therapist needs to be able to understand and work with the unconscious yearnings, internal conflicts, and expectations that underlie the repetitive cycles of conflict in distressed couples, if they are to be effective with many of those presenting for treatment.

Fortunately, there are now a number of conceptual 'maps' to help the therapist understand the psychodynamics of the couple relationship. In this chapter and the next we will introduce the theoretical models and concepts that we have found to be most helpful in fostering our understanding of the unconscious dynamics that play out in the couple. These include the object relations approaches to couple therapy (Clulow & Mattinson, 1989; Dicks, 1967; Ruszczynski, 1993; Scharff & Scharff, 1991; Siegel, 1992), the self-psychological and inter-subjective approaches (Livingston, 2001; Shaddock, 2000; Solomon, 1989), attachment-based models (Bowlby, 1988; Johnson, 1996, 2002), and the relational approach (Mitchell, 2002).

Although all these models emphasize somewhat different aspects of psychoanalytic theory, they share a number of underlying principles. These principles are also central to individual psychoanalytic approaches. However, our focus will be on illuminating how they are relevant to understanding couple dynamics. These core principles include the dynamic unconscious, transference, and how anxiety and defence are played out in the couple relationship.

Underlying principles of psychodynamic approaches to couples

The dynamic unconscious

Within all analytic approaches to couple therapy, the major under-lying principle is that behaviour is determined by unconscious, as well as conscious, motivations, and it is the unconscious motivations that need to be explored and understood to help the couple achieve equilibrium. These unconscious motivations evolve from infancy and childhood, where the developing child builds a 'working model' (Bowlby, 1988) of relationships and how they function. This working model in the child's inner world corresponds with early experiences of parents, siblings, and other caretakers, and the way they have satisfied or frustrated the child's needs and wishes. As Ruszczynski (1993) states,

> Because the infant's emotional and intellectual capacity is very limited, he is unable to apprehend the "reality" of those around him and tends to experience emotions in extreme form. "Good" experiences become idealized and raise the phantasy of omnipo-tence, and "bad" experiences become terrifying and persecutory. This inner world has a compelling reality, and external situations are interpreted in accordance with it. The ways in which the human being relates to his environment and to others in it are characterized by his earliest experiences. . . . However, residues of the more primitive images remain and may be reactivated by certain situations, relationships, or life events. Each new relation-ship throughout life is experienced against the background of these internal images, the more "mature" as well as the more primitive.
>
> (Ruszczynski, 1993, pp. 7—8)

Intimate relationships activate these earlier internal images and experiences in all of us. When this revival of archaic material occurs in a marriage without too much threat to an individual's adult or sexual selves, growth and development can proceed. In such marriages each partner believes that they are held securely enough in the other's love (Cleavely, 1993).

However, when these internalized images derive from overwhelming experiences in childhood, for example neglect or abuse, they are likely to create great difficulty in the couple relationship. Indeed, couple relationships provide an opportunity to begin to deal with the unresolved conflicts of these early relationships. Unconsciously, we are driven to repeat the dynamics of early relationships, in part so that we can get in touch with the experience and find a better way of dealing with it in the present. There can also be a pressure to repeat the dynamics in an attempt to convert the couple relationship into an ideal relationship. The more damaged the early relational experience, the more the couple relationship will need to carry idealized hopes and wishes, which will become increasingly difficult to sustain (Cleavely, 1993). The notion of the *dynamic unconscious* has been used to emphasize the interaction between the dynamics of the current relationship and that of past relationships. There is a lively interaction between conscious and unconscious processes. The unconscious is dynamic in that it constantly seeks expression, normally towards another person who might be able to meet or respond to repressed needs and wishes (Rusczynski, 1993). The unconscious is never fixed, but is in a state of flux, as new relationships modify old templates, and old 'working models' influence new relationships.

Transference

Transference can be understood as the process by which a person's current pattern of relating is unconsciously shaped by their experience in key relationships in earlier life, especially in early childhood. Some of these early relational experiences were what the person needed at the time — 'good enough' experiences, in Winnicott's (1965) memorable phrase — in order to facilitate further emotional development. Other relational experiences were not 'good enough': they were disappointing or were even missing entirely, or were perhaps too overwhelming in terms of the level of excitement or frustration involved, for optimal emotional development. Together, these 'good enough' and 'not good enough' experiences provide a base from which each person develops their own unconscious 'agenda for relationship', the uniquely personal pattern of what the person looks for, expects, fears, and longs for in their adult relationships. This becomes the personal lens through which the person instinctively, *and unconsciously*, perceives and experiences, and therefore manages or organizes, their experience of relationships. What the person unconsciously *expects* to see or to have happen in their relationships will be what they respond to, regardless of the other person's intent; this is especially the case in emotionally significant relationships, or at points where there is uncertainty, anxiety, or tension in the relationship (Grant & Crawley, 2002).

Transference typically occurs when the client unconsciously reacts to the therapist according to these patterns established early in life through interactions with parents and siblings. It includes feelings towards the therapist, expectations about how to behave, and what the client anticipates from the therapist (Grant & Crawley, 2002). For example, the client may expect the therapist to like them or approve of them, to be critical of them, to understand, or to abuse, neglect, or abandon them.

However, transference does not just occur in therapy relationships. It is ubiquitous and also occurs in relationships with partners, friends, lovers, bosses, and others, especially those with some significance or intensity (Balint, 1993; Grant & Crawley, 2002). We unwittingly assume others will respond to us as we have been treated before, particularly by our mother, father, or siblings. We then behave according to those assumptions (Grant, 2000). Because being in a relationship arouses so many unconscious fantasies and expectations, the transference to each other is likely to be very intense. This may include the more positive *idealizing transferences* or more difficult hostile or rejecting transference experiences.

Couples will bring to therapy their more 'focused transference' towards their partner. However, they will also bring a shared contextual transference (Scharff & Scharff, 1991). This shared contextual transference concerns their shared hopes and fears with regard to the therapist's ability to provide therapeutic holding for their couple relationship. We will talk more about focused and contextual transferences in Chapter 7.

Anxiety and defence

The role of anxiety and defence is central to understanding the evolving dynamics of the couple. All of us experience from time to time impulses or feelings that give rise to anxiety; this anxiety, in turn, arouses a *defence* or protective mechanism. Defences help to protect the individual from intolerable anxiety and conflict. They reduce the impact of a threatening experience by moving it from the conscious to the unconscious realm (Grant & Crawley, 2002; Juni, 1997). In this way, defences may protect self-esteem, ward off dangerous sexual or aggressive impulses, or protect the individual from frightening or painful feelings.

In the couple relationship, the defences of projection and projective identification (which will be discussed later in this chapter) are particularly important. With projection, traits and needs such as aggression, ambition, dependency, restrictiveness, and control or lack of control can all be disowned in the self and projected onto the partner (Grant, 2000; Grant & Crawley, 2002). This process can interact with gender identity (Grant & Porter, 1994). For example, a male partner may project his dependency needs onto his female partner and then experiences her as being 'needy'. This defence allows him to distance himself from his own dependency needs and maintain his masculine identity as an autonomous being (Grant, 2000). Positive traits may also be projected. For example, a female partner may project calmness and sensitivity onto her male partner, and then assume that he will carry these qualities for the couple. This protects her from looking at her own insensitivity to others.

Much of couple therapy concerns helping partners to withdraw their projections from each other. Sometimes, these projections are very intense and entrenched. For example, Nick, who is married to Alison, has had a series of affairs. However, he cannot bear the anxiety of looking at the impact of his behaviour on the relationship and instead continually accuses Alison of wanting to leave the marriage and of engaging in extramarital relationships.

Another common defence in couple relationships is to utilize anger, control, withdrawal, and rejection to defend against feelings of sadness and vulnerability. These feelings arouse anxiety that is dealt with by utilizing *secondary emotions* — emotions that cover the *primary emotions* often reactivated from childhood because of the intensity of a couple relationship. For example,

Mary and Don are both young professionals with demanding careers. Mary is frequently enraged with Don because he is often late for either scheduled social activities or dinner at home. In his view, the lateness is due simply to important business pressures and meetings, which he feels unable to exit to meet his other time commitments. He feels that Mary is very controlling and completely unreasonable in her expectations. He would like her to be more understanding of the multiple pressures in his life. Mary, however, feels that the lateness is not just rude, but a clear signal that he does not respect her or care about her needs. She is so enraged by the time he arrives, she attacks him with accusations of self-centredness, deliberate cruelty, and immaturity, and threatens to leave the relationship. This pattern normally escalates, with Don eventually withdrawing by leaving the house. With some gentle exploration in therapy, it emerged that Mary experienced Don's lateness as abandonment, and the later he was, the more distraught she felt. When she was young, Mary had experienced extreme emotional abandonment from both parents, who were too self-absorbed in their careers and glamourous social life to give her very much attention. When she was 15, they had put her in a flat on her own because they felt she was troublesome. Essentially, the primary emotion in Mary was sadness at feeling abandoned by Don; this was defended against by rage at him, part of which belonged with her parents. For Don, Mary's threats to end the relationship were terrifying, because he had been unceremoniously kicked out of home at 17. However, he was not able to express his fear to Mary, but instead protected himself by withdrawing, which enraged her more.

Object relations approaches to couple therapy

A brief overview of the major object relations couples theorists

Henry Dicks (1967) was one of the most influential writers on couple therapy. A psychoanalyst, Dicks applied Fairbairn's (1952; 1963) object relations theory to the couple relationship. His book *Marital Tensions* was based on his work at the Tavistock Clinic in London during the 1950s and 1960s, with predominantly working-class couples. Dicks articulated three subsystems involved in marital choice: (i) public aspects such as social class, ethnicity, and education; (ii) central egos, which focused on aspects such as personal norms, personal choices, conscious expectations, values, and attitudes; and (iii) unconscious fit between the pair, which stressed the *unconscious complementarities* between the partners. He argued that it was difficult for marriages to survive well if there were significant differences in two or more of these subsystems.

At about the same time that Dicks was formulating principles of couple therapy, a separate group at the Tavistock Institute was also experimenting with psychoanalytically informed therapy for couples. Established first in 1948 as the Family Discussion Bureau, this group eventually evolved into what is now known as the Tavistock Centre for Couple Relationships (TCCR) (Ruszczynski, 1993). In their work the TCCR have drawn upon a wide range of analytic theories to help understand couple dynamics, including Freudian, object relations, and Jungian perspectives, and has been highly influential in developing theory and practice in psychodynamic couple therapy.

In the United States, David Scharff and Jill Scharff (1991; 1982) have been the most prominent proponents of object relations therapy with couples, and have developed an International Institute of Object Relations Therapy. Both psychiatrists, who have trained in psychoanalysis, they have integrated material from Fairbairn (1963), Winnicott (1960), Dicks (1967), Ogden (1982), and Racker (1968) in their approach to couple therapy. Also in the United States, Judith Siegel (1992) has made a significant contribution to object relations couple therapy by integrating theory from the American object relations theorists such as Kernberg (1987) and Jacobson (1964), and the self-psychology approach of Kohut (1984). Each of these theorists emphasizes somewhat different aspects of psychodynamic theory; however, our concern here is with introducing the practitioner to some of the core constructs in the object relations approach that are most helpful in thinking about the dynamics in couples, rather than with the finer points of difference between theorists.

Internal object relations

A cornerstone of object relations couples theory is the development of *internal object relations*, which are so important in the unconscious ties between partners. Internal object relations refers to the notion that we have all developed expectations about how to relate to others based on our experiences in the past. Early relationships with parents, siblings, grandparents, and teachers leave their mark in the form of *internal objects* — mental representations of others and ourselves (Dicks, 1967; Donovan, 2003; Scharff & Scharff, 1991; Siegel, 1992). The term 'object' is somewhat unfortunate, but refers to the notion that the other person is a recipient of unconscious needs, conflicts, and wishes that are directed towards them (Ruszczynski, 1993). In this way, the notion of object makes it clear that the experience of another is not simply interpersonal, but also holds an intrapsychic dimension. These images are often not conscious, but nevertheless drive our expectations, responses, and behaviour towards others, particularly in intimate relationships. For example, if we had parents who had high expectations in academic and social areas, and who were highly corrective, we may expect our partner to be critical of less-than-perfect performance and may also judge our own mistakes harshly. We might also expect that love only accompanies achievement in work or social spheres. That is, our internal object would be that of a corrective, critical parent, with accompanying expectations of both others and ourself.

When there is too much anger, anxiety, or guilt, the child *represses* the object relationship into the unconscious (Dicks, 1967). This object relationship includes an affect, an object (another person or part of another person), and a self-representation.

Fairbairn (1952) suggested that the child represses *libidinal object relationships*, those based on frustrating sexual or loving experiences, and *anti-libidinal object relationships*, those based on dangerous, rejecting, abandoning experiences with significant objects. In current theorizing, these are often referred to as the *exciting* and *rejecting* parts of the self and the objects (Scharff & Scharff, 1998). Children repress these object relationships because they are too overwhelming to be integrated into the conscious self. For example, as a young boy, Don feels rage (affect) at being rejected by his contemptuous father (object) and made to feel weak and unlovable (self-representation), but this rejecting experience is too much to bear, so he represses it and thinks about his parents as normal parents who did the best they could.

Dicks (1967) argued that *repressed objects* or *object relationship experiences* re-emerge in the couple relationship, as each partner attempts to get the other to meet the needs which have been repressed from childhood experiences. When Don experiences Mary's contempt with his perennial lateness, he again experiences feeling weak and unlovable, feels rage, and either lashes out at Mary or withdraws. It is as if Mary becomes his contemptuous father who will abandon him. This split-off object relation is still charged with psychic energy, because it has never been worked through enough for it to be part of the conscious ego. Like most repressed object relationship experiences, it pushes through to express the rage involved. Once this process begins, Don feels unable to simply apologize for being late, or hear Mary's distress; in that moment she *is* the contemptuous father who makes him feel week and unlovable.

One of the reasons why this is such a helpful theoretical framework is that it begins to explain some of the desperate intensity of serious couple conflict. Using an example from the libidinal or exciting part of the self, if you are not only fighting for loving tender sexual attention in the present, but also unconsciously trying to get your partner to provide the missing loving attention from your distant absent father, you will fight with a distressed intensity that originates in your fear of abandonment as a child. As a therapist, we often talk to couples about the past experiences adding fuel to the fire, so that what might have been a small blaze that could be easily put out becomes an inferno. It is not that it is all entirely in the past — there are realities in the present relationship too, but the emotional intensity will be much higher if the past is fuelling the present experience of relationship. Through unconscious processes of trans-ference, projection, anxiety, and defence, we tend to recreate our internal world in our relationships, and our more intimate relation-ships will foster greater intensity in re-experiencing that dynamic. This is why individuals who are able to remain rational and calm in other settings can find themselves responding with waves of emo-tional reactivity in their closest relationships (Donovan, 2003).

Marital fit and partner choice

When Dicks (1967) wrote about marital fit, he was most interested in the subsystem that had to do with unconscious complementarities between partners. Using the complex notion of internal object rela-tions, he developed three elegant hypotheses about when uncon-scious couple conflict was most likely to occur:

1. When the partner is chosen because they are like a cherished parent, but then does not match the idealized parental role for which they were selected, eliciting invidious comparisons.
2. When an individual marries a partner because they seem to provide the opposite of a disappointing parent, only to discover that they enact similar dynamics.
3. When the individual sees the repressed or disowned part of themselves in their partner. Although they may have chosen their partner to complement their personality, the qualities they were attracted to in their partner are qualities that are deni-grated in the self, and so may also become denigrated in the other.

Using these principles, Dicks set out to understand the unconscious object relationships causing conflict for the couple. The notion of *unconscious marital fit* — that partners choose others to fit their unconscious internal world — has remained an important concept in understanding couple dynamics (Balint, 1993; Fisher, 1999; Lyons,

1993; Ruszczynski, 1993). Part of this unconscious marital fit has to do with the *internal parental couple* — that is, the partly conscious and partly unconscious internalized picture of the relationship of one's own parents (Fisher, 1999; Scharff & Scharff, 1991). Whether we seek to emulate that relationship or avoid recreating it, the *internal parental couple* forms the basis for strong expectations about how partners should engage with each other.

Partners choose each other both consciously and unconsciously. The unconscious agenda for relationship sometimes has to do with our unconscious need for a second chance to resolve difficulties we could not resolve earlier; at other times it seems more to do with finding someone onto whom we can project — and then identify with — disowned aspects of ourselves (Grant & Crawley, 2002).

Intimacy

Intimacy involves endowing one's partner with an idealized representational world. However, the partner is endowed with the negative parts of the inner representational world, as well as the idealized parts. Because early objects were felt to be magical and all-powerful, this power is transferred to the new object (Siegel, 1992). The partner is then invested with the power to regulate security, self-esteem, and other internal functions as well as the power to reject and abandon. This psychic investment in the other helps to explain the dependency and regression that arise with intimacy. The experience of dependency in a couple relationship often activates strong responses related to early experiences of dependency. Fears of engulfment, abandonment, or being controlled can lead to self-protective attacks on the relationship. The partner will be expected to provide loving resources that may not have been originally provided. The capacity to become truly intimate eventuates when internalized early experiences were sufficiently responsive and validating to allow trust and closeness to emerge (Siegel, 1992).

Intimacy requires that one be able to depend on one's partner and to be depended upon. The inability to depend creates as many problems as excessive dependency. Intimacy requires a *related individuation*, which is the capacity to be close enough to bestow others with important psychological functions, but to remain an individual who can pursue goals and take responsibility for oneself (Siegel, 1992). There is always a tension between independence and dependence in any couple relationship. Maintaining a close connection while pursuing one's own agenda for development is a balance that needs to be addressed recurrently throughout a relationship. As well as dependency, intimacy arouses issues of self-esteem, trust, responsibility, control, autonomy, and self-assertion.

Projective identification

The concept of projective identification is central to all object relations approaches to couple therapy (Ruszczynski, 1993; Scharff & Scharff, 1991; Siegel, 1992). Projective identification goes beyond transference and is considered a core process in couple conflict. Projective identification is an unconscious process that involves an individual projecting a part of the self into another person and then inducing them to behave in accordance with the projection (Scharff & Scharff, 1991; Siegel, 1992; Solomon, 1989). This part can be a good part or a bad part — angry, hostile, persecutory, or contemptible. The receiving person identifies with some aspect of the projection and is induced to behave in accordance with it. But the projecting individual may also begin to identify with what he/she has projected, which may be a part of the self or an aspect of an object; for example, the projection may be a self-representation such as a needy, weak child, or a part of a parental object such as a controlling, angry mother (Fisher, 1999; Scharff & Scharff, 1991). Couples change each other through these processes. What is more, couples usually engage in mutual projective identifications, so that projections go both ways (Scharff & Scharff, 1991; Siegel, 1992). Let us consider an example to clarify this somewhat complicated mechanism.

Amanda is an under-confident 40-year-old with poor self-esteem. She grew up in a family where she was overlooked because of her older sister's closer connection with her mother. Her mother was preoccupied and her father was rarely home, and Amanda grew up with little positive attention or guidance. She married Alex in her twenties, partly because he was confident and self-assured and seemed to know where he was going in life. She now experiences Alex as controlling and as inattentive to her needs for reassurance and positive feedback. Amanda projects her inattentive mother into Alex, and then increasingly begs for reassurance about herself and her capacities. The constant request for reassurance exasperates Alex and induces him to push Amanda away and tell her that he wants her to be more independent. Alex, who is busy building a successful career, partly identifies with the mother, who wanted her daughter to be independent so she could get on with her life, and accuses Amanda of being 'needy'. Amanda then experiences the same loneliness and lack of interest in her that she experienced as a child; in a desperate attempt to engage Alex, Amanda becomes angry and accuses him of being selfish, withholding, and not loving her. The fight about this issue is always intense, with both partners wondering whether they may be better off apart.

It is as if what you are not able to tolerate or are very frightened of in yourself is then located in the other, where it is attacked. These processes help to explain the high degree of emotional reactivity that is often seen in distressed couples. Fisher (1999) outlines two main types of projections: (i) the subjective aspects of the self such as rage, anger, sadism, and persecution; and (ii) the internal objects which consist of figures that inhabit the internal world, such as the internal parental couple, an abusive father, or a self-absorbed mother. He argues that it is the interaction between these subjective aspects and internal objects of the self which leads to an impulse to attack or retaliate. This process can lead to more persistent and sinister projections and counter-projections, leading the couple into a vicious cycle of attack and retaliation. This process can lead to the experience of mutual loathing often seen in couples who cannot part, but who are held together in a shared contempt or hatred (Fisher, 1999; Solomon, 1989). They cannot part because they carry the unacceptable traits for each other and must keep the other close to preserve control.

From an object relations perspective, the central goal of couple therapy is to assist each individual to recognize and reacquire lost parts of themselves that have been projected into the partner (Fisher, 1999; Scharff & Scharff, 1991; Siegel, 1992). This means the individual must work through the conflict internally, and begin to recognize why these aspects of the self are felt to be so intolerable. As this occurs and the projections are reintegrated, there is a better chance that the couple can return to a more balanced position. In this respect, the aim is not to help the couple to solve the external conflict, but to assist them to face the conflict through reintegrating their projections (Fisher, 1999). This is accomplished through interrupting negative destructive cycles and offering an empathic understanding towards the feelings and experiences of each partner (Siegel, 1992). Conflicts will continue, as they do for all couples, but what changes is the ability to tackle the conflicts, understand them, and solve them. Once the projections are reintegrated, the bitter intensity that has previously made the conflict so difficult to resolve is often not there.

Ideally, we might think that when a couple come to a point when they can think together about their emotional experience instead of trying to control the other through intrusive projections or emotional abandonment, they are also ready to be free of the therapy. The couple hopefully have come to a point at which they are able in the dynamics of their relationship to allow the other the kind of emotional freedom that either makes the continued loving presence of the other a gift, or allows the other to leave to form a new relationship.

(Fisher, 1999, p. 283)

Containment and holding

An important concept that guides practice is that of *containment*. The notion is borrowed from Bion (1967), who defines it as the mother's capacity to take in the infant's uncontainable, and therefore projected, experience, think about it, and give it back in a less toxic form. Bion thought this was also what an analyst did for their patient. This is similar to Winnicott's (1960) notion of *holding* or the *holding environment*. However, the holding environment refers more to the consistency, dependability, and responsiveness of the parenting. Both of these concepts are important in couple's therapy (Crawley, 2007). The couple needs both holding and containment. In therapy, the holding environment refers to the structure provided, in terms of regularity of sessions, the timing of session, fees, and the accepting and non-reactive attitude of the therapist. The therapy also provides a temporary container for the couple, where projective identifications can be absorbed and understood rather than repeatedly enacted (Colman, 1993; Scharff & Scharff, 1991; Siegel, 1992). If both partners need continual containment, there will be a struggle over 'who gets to be the baby' (Lyons & Mattinson, 1993). However, one of the important aims of couple therapy is to promote the capacity of the couple relationship to function as a psychological container for each of the partners (Colman, 1993) until the container function of the marital relationship can be restored (Fisher, 1999).

Countertransference

For the object relations couple therapist, therapy is primarily about understanding the internal world of the couple through their mutual projective processes (Scharff & Scharff, 1991; Siegel, 1992). Therapists share their thinking with the couple through interpretations, explanations, and non-judgemental acceptance. They watch the couple closely over a number of sessions to identify the unconscious forces that propel the repetitive patterns that keep the couple stuck. In order to do this, they use their own *countertransference* to the couple and the individual partners as the best guiding beacon to these unconscious processes.

The Scharff & Scharff (1991) have emphasized, articulated, and detailed this process most fully. They describe how they notice and make sense of their own emotional responses, images, and fantasies of the individuals and the couple in order to fully understand the couple dynamic. They pay attention to how the couple deals with the therapist and also the impact of the couple interaction on the therapist. Using their own personal and professional experience with couples — their parents, friends, prior relationships, therapeutic relationships — they seek to understand the patterns in this particular couple.

> Gradually we become familiar with the defensive aspects of these repeating cycles. We do this over and over, covering the same ground and making inroads into defended territory, which we find particularly accessible at times when the couple's transference has stirred a countertransference response through which we can appreciate the couple's vulnerability. As trust builds, we can help the couple figure out and face the nameless anxiety behind the defence. Our help comes in the form of interpretations of resistance, defence and conflict, conceptualized as operating through unconscious object relation systems that support and subvert the marriage.
>
> (Scharff & Scharff, 1991, p. 104)

Sexuality and the psychosomatic partnership

Most psychodynamic couple therapists work actively to understand the couple's sexual relationship. Winnicott (1960) talked about the *psychosomatic partnership* of the infant—mother couple. Borrowing Winnicott's term, the Scharff & Scharff (1991) have shown how the adult couple also has a psychosomatic partnership. This partnership has its origins in the mother—infant relationship, where emotional and physical closeness are united. This very close emotional, physical, loving, nurturing relationship is then replicated within the adult couple sexual relationship. The sexual relationship is the place where the physical interaction of the couple resonates with the couple and individual internal object relationships. The psychosomatic partnership needs to foster 'good-enough sex'; that is, it needs to express intimacy, contain frustration, be a tension-reducing good-enough part of the relationship, while at times meeting the couple's needs and fantasies. The concept of good-enough is helpful — it does not need to be perfect or meet all expectations, but needs to be a satisfying, intimate activity for at least some of the time.

The Scharff & Scharff (1991) argue that the sexual relationship renews the energy in the dyad, repairs wear and tear of ordinary life, and expresses loving aspects of internal object worlds. When it is good, it supports the mutual holding in a couple. However, when it is problematic, it also can amplify repressed internal objects — both rejecting ones and exciting but frustrating ones. In this case, it then attacks the sense of loving, nurturing, and safety in the relationship. Because sexual expression is guided more by unconscious than conscious forces, it is often a difficult area in which to foster change. The Scharff & Scharff suggest that a difficult sexual relationship is usually the result of object relations problems, but that an unsatisfying sexual partnership adds a further burden to the couple relationship, creating a self-reinforcing negative cycle.

The Oedipal drama in the couple relationship

Although object relations theory has been primarily concerned with how early relationships with others are internalized and then replayed in the couple relationship, attention is also given to how the later Oedipal conflicts replay themselves in the couple relationship. In the original Greek myth, the parents of Oedipus order that their infant be murdered to preserve themselves (Grier, 2005). Oedipus is saved by others and grows up; as a young man he unknowingly murders his father and marries his mother. Freud used this myth as a metaphor to understand the passions of the young child for the parent of the opposite sex and the envy aroused in the child by the other parent who has an exclusive sexual relationship with the adored parent. Essentially, the Oedipal conflict is about the anxieties of the triangle, which for a child have to do with being excluded from the parental couple or overly included with one or other of the parents (Fisher, 1999). The myth of Oedipus indicates how complicated, and sometimes how devastating, going from two to three can be.

As an adult, of course, one of the most common disruptions to the couple relationship is the arrival of children. Again, the anxieties are around inclusion and exclusion. Will the new baby take all of the mother's love with none left for the father? Will the child need to be distanced in order to preserve the couple relationship? When the mother sees her husband smiling lovingly at his infant daughter, does it arouse pangs of envy? The arrival of a child is unconsciously connected to the earliest experiences of love, hate, disappointment, and rivalry with parents and siblings (Fisher, 1999; Grier, 2005). The Oedipal drama is about this triangular space, which requires the individual to face the disturbance that comes with being excluded from the parental couple as well as being part of a couple that excludes another (Fisher, 1999).

> Frank was the eldest, with four younger sisters. He always felt like he did not belong and found it difficult to establish his own masculine interests as a child. His father was physically abusive and only interested in whether Frank would achieve in sports. Frank fell in love with Doris, who was very loving and responsive to Frank's needs for a close, connected relationship where he felt he belonged. The relationship was strong until after the arrival of their baby, Jessica. Doris loved being a mother and devoted a great deal of her energy to parenting Jessica. Frank felt miserable and on the outer edge of the family. He did not know how to join in the close dyad of mother and baby and felt continually excluded from the mother—daughter partnership. This had felt so devastating that he was now thinking of leaving the marriage.

However, rather than a baby, the third party may be an important friendship, intense interest, sustained focus on work, or an affair. Like a symbolic child, it can threaten closeness, intimacy, and exclusiveness, and engender envy, hatred, and jealousy (Balfour, 2005; Grier, 2005). These experiences will be connected with the earliest experiences of rivalry, love, and hate with parents and siblings. These experiences can promote development in the couple or be experienced as catastrophic, much like the original tale of Oedipus Rex (Fisher, 1999; Grier, 2005).

> Susan and Tony have entered therapy to deal with the impact of an infidelity of Tony's. The infidelity occurred on only one occasion and was not associated with any ongoing attachment to the woman. Tony was horrified with what he had done and was willing to do anything to repair the damage to the relationship. The relationship was a very loving, solid marriage of 20 years'

duration, and neither partner had been unfaithful before. Susan found it extremely difficult to understand what had happened and was ready to leave the marriage, as a defensive manoeuvre to prevent any further possibility of hurt. Susan's experience of the breach of the marital boundary was explored and processed with the couple over a number of sessions. When the therapist enquired into Susan's experiences in her family of origin, it eventuated that Susan was the eldest of two girls and her younger sister was her mother's favourite. Because her father was frequently absent from the home, Susan could not turn to him for a different kind of relationship. She was often lonely as a child and felt 'unlovable and unchosen'. Although this was painful material to process, it helped Susan to understand how devastating the marital breach had been for her. She had projected an idealized loving connection onto the couple relationship, and in this she was lovable, loved, and chosen — and the only one. The infidelity punctured this picture and aroused old feelings of despair, hatred, and envy.

An additional dynamic is common in the couple relationship. This has to do with individuals feeling caught between fears of engulfment and fears of abandonment. These dynamics originate in the negotiation of the Oedipal situation — how close it is safe for one to be to a mother or father and will they be taken over — engulfed or swallowed up — if they are too close? Can one parent be used to moderate the intensity of the love relationship with the other? These threats, when unresolved, are then replayed in the couple relationship and can produce a deadly quality of desperation and the threat of annihilation in the consulting room (Balfour, 2005).

Gail and Max struggle with issues of closeness and distance. Max would like far more time alone together, while Gail is keen to pursue other friendships and activities separately. Gail was raised in an intense, enmeshed household where her attempts to differentiate herself were met with anxiety and cloying attention. What feels close enough for Max to meet his needs for intimacy feels like engulfment to her.

Of course, the consulting room itself is a triangular space, with the couple and the therapist. This can provoke strong feelings of inclusion, exclusion, and envy in each of the three individuals, including the therapist, as different configurations of closeness, intimacy, and understanding evolve.

Conclusion

The major aim of an object relations approach to couple therapy is to assist couples to become aware of their own conflicted self-images, thereby lessening the projection of them onto their partners. An underlying assumption is that the couple relationship creates the condition for intensive attachment which activates some of the good and bad experiences of early childhood. This approach to therapy operates through a non-judgemental, accepting space where the couple can explore the current conflict and its link with earlier conflicted relationships. The major interventions are an empathic stance, containment, processing of emotional experiences, and understanding of unconscious object relations — often through the therapist's countertransference and interpretation.

2

THE PSYCHODYNAMICS OF THE COUPLE RELATIONSHIP: SELF PSYCHOLOGY, INTERSUBJECTIVITY, AND ATTACHMENT THEORY

Whereas object relations emphasizes the projections and projective identifications of partners, self-psychological and intersubjective approaches place their primary focus on empathically understanding what happens when current or archaic needs are expressed and the partner does not respond as desired. One of the elements that distinguishes self psychology from other analytic approaches is the degree of emphasis on empathic immersion in the detailed exploration of the subjective experience of each partner (Livingston, 1995; 2001).

Empathic immersion

Empathic immersion is 'the capacity to think and feel oneself into the inner life of another person' (Kohut, 1984, p. 82). The first task for the therapist in this approach is a thorough empathic exploration of each partner's subjective experience of the relationship (Shaddock, 2000). This functions as both an assessment tool and a potent intervention; it models to the couple that each partner's experience is important and that there can be a space for different subjective realities (Livingston, 2001; Shaddock, 2000). Careful exploration of each person's experience without judgement produces a lowering of defences. As each partner feels deeply listened to, understood, and responded to by the therapist, they begin slowly to feel safe enough to allow unacknowledged needs, fears, and vulnerabilities to emerge.

The therapist works hard to create a safe environment where the couple can come to accept the message that no one is to blame here and if we keep exploring we will together understand what has happened in the relationship. Couples are anxious when they come to treatment. They hope to be understood and long to draw on the therapist's strength and wisdom, but dread feeling criticized, shamed, or misunderstood (Shaddock, 2000). Essentially, the task of the therapist is to move back and forth slowly exploring each partner's experience in the relationship and offering an empathic response to the underlying feelings and fears of each person. If the partners are volatile, this can be a very difficult process. Couples come for therapy because they have not been able to receive the empathic responsiveness and safety that they need in the relationship. In addition, they often feel hurt and bitter and unable to repair the ruptures in their relationship (Livingston, 2001). Their experience of the therapist, working hard to non-defensively understand, gives them an alternative model of being with their partner's anger, distress, or fear.

Empathic immersion does not imply condoning the behaviour. It is important for the therapist to set limits to behaviours such as tantrums, blaming, and abuse, which are inherently destructive. For example, it is useful to say, 'I will do everything I can to understand your anger, but the way you are expressing it is only distancing me and your partner' (Shaddock, 2000).

Selfobject experiences and transferences

Selfobject experiences entail feeling deeply connected to another person who assists in regulating affect, safety, and self-esteem. The need for them is present from birth and does not disappear, but rather evolves from rigid archaic forms (not just any mother will do) into the more flexible capacities for selfobject relatedness in adulthood. An important aspect to these selfobject experiences is the degree of control that is unconsciously assumed over them. At moments of selfobject relatedness, the other is not experienced as a separate being but rather as an extension of the self, much as one might relate to a part of one's own body. Thus disturbances in the smooth operation of selfobject functioning by the other are acutely registered, and provoke in the infant, or the wounded adult, the kind of anxiety, distress, and rage one might feel if one's right arm suddenly took on a life of its own.

Mother—infant research clearly shows how mutual regulation occurs through both verbal and non-verbal engagement and how this experience of selfobject relatedness is internalized in the developing self (Beebe & Lachman, 1992). A healthy sense of self includes a sense of cohesion, continuity over time, agency, and affect states of vitality and positive self-esteem (Shaddock, 2000). *Selfobject* experience in the couple relationship refers to being able to utilize the other as a source of maintenance, restoration, or consolidation of the internal experience of self. Kohut (1984) said that 'A good marriage is one in which one partner or the other rises to the challenge of providing the selfobject function that the other's temporarily impaired sense of self needs at a particular moment' (p. 200). Or, as he quipped later, it is a place where only one partner goes crazy at a time.

Kohut (1984) argued that three particular forms of selfobject experiences are needed throughout life. The first selfobject need is that of *mirroring*. Mirroring provides responsiveness to self states of pride, expansiveness, excitement, and mastery. Couples have an intense need to obtain this kind of response from each other. If the pleasure in achievement cannot be shared because it elicits a competitive, resentful, or withdrawn response from the other, there will be an intense hunger to have this mirrored by others (Livingston, 2001; Shaddock, 2000). For example,

> Richard, a highly successful businessman has experienced his wife Catherine as disinterested in his achievements and unable to share his delight in some of the public events which have confirmed his importance in his field. He feels very alone and isolated in the relationship and has sought the admiring gaze that he longs for through several affairs with women in his industry. He feels that they are able to 'understand the significance of my achievements and how I have influenced this field'.

The second form of selfobject needs is that of *idealizing*. For young children, this is an extremely important experience of being able to be connected to someone wiser and more powerful than oneself who can help to regulate fear and pain though soothing activity. For couples, there is a need for the partner to provide a soothing, containing, calm presence when anxiety, vulnerability, and distress have overwhelmed the normal capacity for self-regulation (Livingston, 2001; Shaddock, 2000). The partner temporarily provides the calming functions and this means that there can be a return to a more modulated state of self. Although these needs for stability and safety are central to a well-functioning couple relationship, they need to be balanced with the more growth-promoting function that mirroring provides.

re dealing & Mirroring both need to be present in o'ship

For example, Catherine is very hurt because she feels she has provided a safe, secure base for Richard to explore from. However, Richard feels stifled because the safe base has precluded promotion of developmental experiences that would help each of them grow.

The third form of selfobject need is that of *twinship*. Twinship provides a sense of belonging. For the couple relationship, this depends on a sense of likeness in values, tastes, and habits (Shaddock, 2000). It is a struggle for many couples to find activities that they both enjoy; tastes in films, books, sports, holidays, cars, restaurants, food must all be negotiated. If there is too great a difference, this can provoke feelings of isolation and alienation that can lead to disruptions in the couple bond.

Couple relationships reactivate conscious and unconscious memories of archaic selfobject experiences together with the hope for provision of what was faulty or missing in the parental responses (Shaddock, 2000; Solomon, 1989). In times of stress, for example, idealizing selfobject needs are paramount. In healthy couple relationships, there are experiences of being heard, understood, or protected. Similarly, the expansive excited affects are often mirrored in the sexual relationship (Shaddock, 2000). These functions allow couples to overcome great adversity such as illness, death of a child, or financial difficulties. If the relationship can be experienced as a haven in a difficult world, marital satisfaction is usually high (Solomon, 1989).

The essential question is whether the partner feels validated and understood, or abandoned, by his partner's responses and whether the experience of selfobject failure has an archaic component. An intimate couple relationship allows for regression and for selfobject transferences, based on unfulfilled childhood needs, to emerge. Frequently, the longed-for responses originate in the smallest most dependent aspects of the self. Messages such as 'love all of me', 'understand what I need', and 'make a place for my emotions, especially those I cannot accept in myself' are the silent plea behind much couple conflict (Solomon, 1989). Partners need help in recognizing and accepting each other's immature needs. Often when couples seek therapy, it is because they have not been able to provide the selfobject functions for each other. As Kilian (1993) quips, much couple conflict is about who gets to be the 'self' and who gets to be the 'selfobject'.

Narcissistic vulnerability, injury, and rage

Narcissistic vulnerability is an unprotected state of self that lies underneath most defensive behaviour (Livingston, 2001). When there is a repeated childhood pattern of early emotional failures and injuries, this creates narcissistic vulnerability and defensive patterns in subsequent relationships (Solomon, 1989). Injuries that evoke shame or humiliation will cause a range of defensive manoeuvres. Individuals with intense narcissistic vulnerabilities long for involvement in a relationship but have expectations of what their partner can give them which inevitably lead to great disappointment. At the extreme end, there is a fear of fragmentation or internal emptiness. Partners can enact their narcissistic vulnerability through affairs, addictions, and rage. For example, an affair may function to protect a vulnerable individual from being in a marriage that is experienced as too intimate. Behaviour that is difficult to understand acquires meaning when it is understood as an attempt to protect a more fragile self from feelings of overwhelming anxiety, stress, and terror (Livingston, 2001; Solomon, 1989).

Solomon (1989) argues that most relationship issues such as money, work, sex, and parenting are really manifestations of narcissistic vulnerability and narcissistic injuries to self-image. Where there is no history of severe narcissistic injury, differences can be resolved through compromise, negotiation, and acceptance. When there is a history where there was significant failure in providing emotional supplies to the developing child, small issues and arguments can cause experience of fragmentation, rage, and emotional destruction. Some narcissistically vulnerable individuals have expectations of control over their partners as if the partner were an extension of the self.

Narcissistic rage is seen not as an inherent aggressive drive, as in object relations, but as a product of a fragmenting self in response to narcissistic injury (Livingston, 1998). This is different to anger and healthy assertiveness that is the expression of a more cohesive self. Rage often emerges when the partner is not responsive enough to the other who needs affirming, mirroring, soothing, or joining. It is also considered a defence against painful affects such as distress, desperation, abandonment, and helplessness (Livingston, 2001; Solomon, 1989).

Working with narcissistic rage requires the therapist to accept and interpret aggression as an understandable reaction to actual or fantasized slights. The couple therapist might enquire about what it feels like to be so angry. The work is directed towards understanding and regulating affect, rather than correcting distortions (Livingston, 1998). The therapist's role is to focus on feelings, fears, and dangerous impulses in terms of how they happened in earlier life, what activates them in the present and how they can be contained

(Solomon, 1989). The goal is to focus on the underlying vulnerability of each partner, particularly when conflict arises. The therapist needs to remain attuned to each partner and provide a description that includes the subjective experiences of both, while moving towards creating a shared reality. There is an important skill in being able to note the empathic breaks that evoke the rage and then to explore the internal experience of disintegration. A major aim is to assist individuals to develop ways of tolerating vulnerability without recourse to aggression (Livingston, 2001). It is also helpful for the therapist to strengthen the attachment through assisting the couple to repair emotional disruptions with each other (Shaddock, 2000).

Intersubjectivity

The intersubjective approach within psychoanalysis is closely aligned with self psychology. It places a greater emphasis on the contributions of the therapist to the co-construction of the intersubjective space between therapist and client (Atwood & Stolorow, 1984). Within couple therapy, the intersubjective approach contributes the notion that individual experience is embedded in a relationship system, and cannot be understood without understanding how the system operates. Couple relationships are seen as systems of mutual regulation. There will be unsuccessful regulation when one partner ignores or amplifies the other's affects, leading to patterns of escalation of conflict or withdrawal. This then makes it difficult for the partners to use the relationship as a source of soothing for disturbing affects either one experiences.

Within a couple relationship there are unconscious hopes that the relationship will foster new development-enhancing experiences, while at the same time unconscious fears that the old traumatic development-inhibiting experiences will be repeated (Shaddock, 2000). The therapist needs to sensitively explore the issue of what moved the relationship from being organized by positive expectations of the other to one where fears of repetition of childhood trauma dominate. In this sense, there is a search for the event or experience that reorganized the relationship along defensive lines.

One of the key components within intersubjective theory is that psychic reality is context-dependent and needs to be understood within the developmental, relationship, and treatment environments that shape it (Shaddock, 2000). This is somewhat different to some of the assumptions underlying object relations theory which emphasize the fixed self and object internal representations derived from

Intersubjectivity chant here & now exp.
more then object rep's that work
w. doc'hood exp.

childhood experiences. Even where couples seemed locked into an entrenched pattern of blaming and attack, intersubjective approaches focus on how the current relationship is sustaining negative experiences and behaviours.

Treatment goals

Treatment in the self-psychological and intersubjective models of couple therapy focuses on the couple's need for mirroring and idealizing twinship experiences from each other. Since these needs give rise to intense transference—countertransference interactions, the therapist concentrates primarily on the couple's experience of each other and the empathic failures that are generated rather than the relationship with the therapist, more typical of individual approaches (Livingston, 1998; 2001). Part of this work is helping the couple to reshape their negative internal representations of their partner (Solomon, 1989). The emphasis here is not so much on projective identifications, as with object relations therapy, but on understanding what happens when archaic needs are expressed and the partner does not give the hoped-for response.

Much of the intervention is aimed at careful exploration of the emotions that lie below the surface of their conflicts. The exploration gives a message that each partner is to be heard and will not be blamed, attacked, or shamed by the therapist. This also provides a model of empathic attunement until they can begin to provide such experiences for each other (Shaddock, 2000; Solomon, 1989). There is an emphasis on working with present perceived selfobject disappointments, as well as archaic ones. However, there is also a focus on helping the couple to learn to tolerate a relationship composed of both successes and failures in selfobject function. In addition, individuals may need to work through their archaic longings for merger originating in the experience of the mother of infancy. These deep longings are met again during the 'in love' state and during sexual union, but are not continuously sustainable in an adult relationship.

The empathic immersion in each partner's experience helps to contain anxiety while helping each person to own and integrate feelings. This is largely done through a translation of blaming and attacking behaviour into meaningful messages about needs and fears in the relationship. The therapist suggests that they stay with feelings rather than attack or blame the other. The therapist slows down the process and asks questions such as 'what just occurred is painful — what do you normally do when it feels too much to tolerate?' or 'what feelings do you have that resonate with what your partner just said — how do you protect yourself against feelings that are too painful?' (Solomon, 1989). The goal is to help the couple to engage in self-observation when hurt, anger, or humiliation occurs, rather than projecting blame onto the other — or to be curious rather than furious about differences (Shaddock, 2000). Differences arouse deep fears of either annihilation (I may be taken over by your differences) or abandonment (we may not have any connection).

Within the self-psychological/intersubjective models, partners are assisted to balance *responsiveness* and *reactiveness* (Livingston, 2001). Responsivity is a mode of listening from an empathic stance towards the partner's experience. But to do this one must be able to de-centre from one's own emotional reactions. Reactivity is a mode of listening from one's own emotional perspective (Bacal, 1998). For example, if couples can allow the other to express anger without reacting with anger of their own, there is a possibility of working through the anger rather than an escalation of it. Occasionally it may enhance therapy to introduce a task for the couple, such as a reflective listening exercise to create mirroring experiences, or encouraging self-assertion through asking partners to articulate what kind of relationship they want. For example, 'I'd like to see if you can really get her to understand what you are wanting from her.'

In summary, the key curative factor is the investigation and legitimization of the underlying vulnerability of each partner's self (Livingston, 1998). The major focus on empathic immersion differentiates self psychology from other analytic approaches. Conflict is not avoided, but it is explored and understood as a break in the empathic tie between the partners. Self psychology attempts to strengthen affect regulation, containment, self-cohesion, and intimacy (Livingston, 2001). When each partner feels deeply understood in their vulnerability, they can begin to develop a much deeper intimate connection with each other. In essence, the therapist needs to be

> attuned to both partners' subjective experience . . . acknowledge their individual and sometimes conflicting selfobject needs . . . function as a selfobject . . . empathically comment on and relate to the needs underlying the dysfunctional interactions and the defensive patterns . . . interpret the connection between past and present . . . and to contain destructive behaviour . . . by setting limits and providing structure.
>
> (Goldstein, 1997, pp. 75—76)

Attachment theory and couple therapy

Although attachment theory uses somewhat different explanatory mechanisms, it overlaps considerably with self-psychological and inter-subjective approaches in terms of its explication of the underlying causes of marital distress. Both self-psychological/intersubjective approaches and attachment-based approaches are predominantly concerned with how protest, anger, and withdrawal are used as defensive manoeuvres to protect an underlying fear or vulnerability in the couple system.

The attachment framework was developed by John Bowlby (1958; 1973) to account for the way that individuals form emotional bonds with significant others and how psychological disturbances such as depression and anxiety are linked with disruption to those bonds. Bowlby showed how attachment provides mechanisms of safety and protection for the growing child and how separation and loss disturbs this 'secure base' or 'safe haven', generating protest and anger, depression, resignation, and detachment. Attachment helps to regulate proximity to caregivers, which enables exploration of the environment (secure base) while providing a safe retreat in times of illness, fatigue, or stress (safe haven). Disruption of attachment generates powerful and primitive emotions.

Attachment theory assumes that such early experiences become internally organized into a 'working model' (Bowlby, 1973) of relationships that become the foundation of later adult personality. Such working models include the complex network of emotions, cognitive representations, and behaviour in relationships — in essence, a map of the self and its relationship to others. Individuals unconsciously use the model to predict, understand, and make meaning of current relationships.

Good attachment experiences in childhood provide safety, security, and protection. The function is the same in adulthood — the formation of enduring bonds with a few significant others that can be counted on for psychological protection, reassurance, and restoration of equilibrium, leading to a secure attachment pattern (Sable, 2000; Johnson, 2002). Poor attachment experiences lead to insecure attachment patterns, which are associated with a range of disturbances including anxiety disorders, depression, eating disorders, and personality disorders (Sable, 2000).

Individual strategies in relationships

Attachment theory offers a way of conceptualizing the client's attachment experiences and how the effects of early events have influenced the 'working models' the individual uses about relationships (Fosha, 2000; Sable, 2000). Whereas secure attachment experiences lead to unconscious beliefs that others are available, understanding and responsive (Fonagy, 2001), insecure attachment experiences lead to unconscious beliefs that significant others are unavailable and unresponsive, or rejecting, abandoning, and abusive. Further, the child learns to deny any aspects of its experience that their caregiver cannot tolerate in order to hold on to the bond. These denied experiences and feelings then become off-limit, leading to a restricted range of affects in relational experiences in adulthood (Fosha, 2000).

Individuals search unconsciously for a partner who can somehow 'fit' or tolerate their internal working model, with the hope that old patterns can be mastered. Understanding these strategies assists therapists to formulate therapeutic goals for couples — helping clients to come to a more balanced position — not too distant and not dependently close to each other.

Louise and Linda had been together about a year, but could not seem to take the next step of moving in together or committing to a long-term relationship, even though each said this was what she wanted. This impasse brought them into couple therapy.

At the start of the relationship Linda was attracted to the spontaneity in Louise and her ease with expressing and understanding her own emotional life. Louise, in turn was attracted to Linda's thoughtful, careful approach to life and her capacity to plan, invest, and save for the future. They also had many shared interests and fully enjoyed their leisure time together.

However, Linda was extremely cautious because she had been badly hurt in a previous relationship and was uncertain of her capacity to stand up for herself in a full-time relationship, especially with someone as emotionally articulate as Louise. In spite of being extremely competent in the public world, with a good job, a house she owned, and investments for the future, she was emotionally very vulnerable. She needed a great deal of quiet space to recover from being with others, including Louise.

Linda grew up as an only child in a family with a very invasive mother, who wanted to control most aspects of Linda's life. Because her father worked long hours and was largely absent from the home, Linda had no recourse to another source of protection or sustenance. Being with her mother meant doing what her mother wanted her to do. Linda was the primary focus of her mother's energies and her success at school and in sport was key to her mother's sense of self-esteem. Although Linda loved her mother, she found it impossible to stand up to her or to establish her own sense of identity. She dealt with this by becoming increasingly secretive and closed off from her mother's emotionality.

Louise, on the other hand, had the experience of abandonment by both her mother and father. She was neglected by both and by 15 was moved into an apartment with her brother and nanny, so her parents could move in with other partners. She would panic as Linda moved away from her, and as she tried to repair the gap, Linda would panic as Louise tried to move closer.

With some work, these dynamics were uncovered and this allowed Louise and Linda to make more conscious choices about how they were going to manage their fears about being together in a relationship. Louise began to understand Linda's need for quiet and privacy and not read it as rejection of her. Linda in turn was more able to move closer to Louise when she realized that Louise would not manipulate her into doing things her way the way her mother had. It is worth noting that on the surface, this was a couple who got along well, had good communication skills with each other, played well together, and clearly asserted they wanted to take the relationship to the next step. On a conscious level, there was nothing impeding the progress of the relationship. But on an unconscious level, each was creating a cycle of interaction that pulled unconscious fears and panic from the other so that they could not create the trusting relationship they each needed to form a more solid attachment, to trust at a deeper level, and to take the step towards commitment.

This anecdote also illustrates the process of working with a same-sex couple and their desire for intimacy and a long-term, committed relationship. In our experience a common issue for same-sex couples has to do with 'sameness' and its attendant features of over-familiarity, boredom, and lack of sexual passion. One way to counteract this is to commit to someone very different, in terms of either personality (like the above example), race, culture, or class.

Narrative competence and reflective function

Couple therapy assists clients to recapture memories and express feelings that have been disallowed in previous relationships. This, in turn, helps clients to create a more coherent narrative or unified vision of themselves — a 'story' about the self (Holmes, 2001; Sable, 2000). Therapy also provides an accepting relationship which can validate experiences and enable clients to alter their internal representations so that they become more capable of mutually supportive relationships (Sable, 2000). Indeed, the capacity to construct a coherent narrative about oneself and one's difficulties is directly linked to secure attachment and the capacity for mutuality in relationship.

Couple therapy also encourages the capacity known as *reflective function* or *mentalization* (Fonagy, 2001). Reflective function is the capacity to reflect on one's own and others' mental states; it is highly correlated with secure attachment and psychological health. In the same way, the therapist has a 'thinking mind' — using it to think about and put words to what might be going on in each of the partners' minds (Fonagy, 2001; Holmes, 2001).

In couple relationships, it is often this need to *have a place in the mind of the other* that underlies many conflicts around practical things like time spent together. For example,

Gavin and Kirsten have reached a mutually acceptable compromise, where Kirsten spends time alone at parties and large social gatherings — occasions Gavin does not enjoy. However, Gavin finds it difficult to relax when Kirsten is out — especially if she stays out late, instead experiencing sleep deprivation and high anxiety. His therapist offered an interpretation: 'When Kirsten stays out till all hours of the morning without letting you know when she will return, it feels like she is not holding you and your needs in mind. I wonder if this feels somewhat like the relationship with your mother who was overburdened and could not hold your needs as primary?' Gavin responded to this with some relief that his therapist had understood the underlying disturbance and was able to use the insight to explain to Kirsten what was going on for him.

The therapeutic relationship: Secure base and safe haven

Attachment theory provides useful explanations for how couples psychotherapy works. Therapists provide a stable warm relationship, firm boundaries, handling of protest, reliability, and emotional responsiveness that assists with affect regulation — all elements of a secure attachment bond (Bowlby, 1988; Holmes, 2001; Mallinckrodt et al., 1995). This secure base can be gradually internalized by clients so that the presence of the therapist is no longer needed. Psychotherapy can also provide a 'safe haven' — a place of refuge when emotional experiences overwhelm the couple.

The 'transitional space' between partners

Attachment theory and research is concerned with both the inter-personal and the intrapsychic world. It focuses on the space between self and other and how that is represented in the inner world. Such 'transitional space' (Winnicott, 1971) is where the parents help the child to make meaning of experience. For example, the baby points and the parent responds with 'yes, you can see a cat', or babbling and emotion are 'storied' for the child. It is also the space where what the baby or child means to the mother/father is expressed through their responses, gestures, and facial expressions.

We have written elsewhere about this transitional space and its importance in the couple relationship (Grant & Crawley, 2001; Crawley & Grant, 2001). Like the play space between mother and baby, it is where inner and outer realities of each partner can coexist so that there can be reflection and dialogue about self and other. This transitional space can easily become constricted in distressed couples. As experience in therapy is absorbed, it modifies the internal working model of each partner (Aron, 1996; Grant & Crawley, 2001). This, in turn, has the potential to transform the relationship as each partner begins to perceive the other differently, modify their relational beha-viours, and thus expand the transitional space (Grant & Crawley, 2001).

Attachment theory and the couple relationship

Attachment theory helps us to understand the couple relationship in terms of the attachment styles each partner uses and the systemic interaction between different styles. One very useful model is pro-vided by Bartholomew, Henderson & Dutton (2001). Using Bowlby's analysis of the internal working models, they have generated four prototypic attachment patterns in adulthood that are underpinned by two dimensions (Figure 2.1).

- *Secure attachment* leads to a positive view of self and other. Secure individuals can establish close relationships and use others as support when needed.
- *Preoccupied attachment* leads to a positive model of other, but negative model of self, eliciting a demanding and dependent style.

Positive model of other

SECURE

Comfortable with
intimacy and autonomy
in close relationships.

PREOCCUPIED

Preoccupied with close
relationships. Overly
dependent on others for
self-esteem and support.

*Positive
model of self*

*Negative
model of self*

DISMISSING

Down-plays importance
of close relationships.
Compulsive self-reliance.

FEARFUL

Fearful of intimacy due
to fear of rejection.
Socially avoidant.

Negative model of other

Figure 2.1 Two-dimensional, four-category model of adult attachment
(Bartholomew et al., 2001).

- *Fearful attachment* is that in which others are viewed as uncaring
  and the self as unlovable. Intimacy is avoided because rejection is
  expected.
- *Dismissing attachment* leads individuals to distance themselves
  from others to maintain a positive view of self. Compulsive self-
  reliance and self-control offers protection from rejection.

These are ideal types; most people would have a predominant style,
but in particular circumstances might resort to one of the other
strategies.

In healthy couple relationships, each partner is able to move
reciprocally between the depended upon and the dependent positions. With insecure attachment styles, individuals are often more
fixed in one position, unable to ask for support or provide it in a
mutually enhancing manner.

Love and the relational approaches

Whereas attachment theory focuses on how threats to the attachment
bond disrupt the couple relationship, making it feel unsafe, other
theorists argue that the capacity to take emotional risks is as

important as the capacity to create safety in a relationship. Stephen Mitchell has been an eloquent spokesperson for relational approaches to psychoanalysis, most recently applying these understandings to couple dynamics (Mitchell, 2002). He argues that at the centre of many marital difficulties are the couple's struggle to integrate desire and love. This struggle emanates from two competing forces within us — that for *safety* and that for *adventure*. Mitchell (2002) persuasively shows how we work to make love safe by making it secure and predictable. However, we then experience our relationship as unexciting and lifeless. The sexual relationship is central to this struggle: 'What makes intense desire, sexual and otherwise, so dangerous is that it entails a longing for something important from a unique someone whom one has allowed to become important. It is the specificity of the other that leads to risk, the allure of another subject outside one's control that creates such intense vulnerability' (Mitchell, 2002, pp. 86—87). Then, in order to protect our vulnerability, we seek control over the love object, trying to make them predictable and dependable. In meeting our strong needs for a safe attachment with our partner, we are inclined to forego risk and novelty — the essence of eroticism. However, bringing our conflicting desires to the person on whom we depend can be considerably riskier than fantasizing about others or indeed expressing our fantasies to others who we do not depend on for emotional security.

Mitchell argues that the fading of romantic love over time has less to do with familiarity than with the risk of allowing 'episodic passionate idealization' (p. 114) in the relationship you depend on for security. It is this risk of sustaining desire for someone so significant that feels most dangerous in marital emotional life. However, keeping the erotic alive is dependent on this capacity to occasionally celebrate the best in the other.

While desire seeks experiences of adventure and surrender, love seeks continuity and stability. 'In love we are searching for points of attachment, anchoring, something we know we can count on. In desire we are searching both for missing, disowned pieces of ourselves and for something beyond ourselves, outside the borders of self-recognition that, under ordinary circumstances, we protect so fiercely' (Mitchell, 2002, p. 92).

Mitchell also elucidates the connection between aggression and desire in useful ways. Aggression should not be avoided, but contained alongside love. Like Dicks (1967), he sees hate and love as inevitably intertwined in long-term relationships. Indeed, the capacity to sustain a loving relationship over time requires that couples survive and repair hate. Both dependency and aggression are needed for romantic passion, within which passion 'needs space for aggression to breathe' (Mitchell, 2002, p. 142). However, aggression can also be used to keep things stable and predictable. For example, continual contempt for one's partner may be a way of trying to maintain control over the object of love.

Mitchell's theorizing about love, desire, and aggression in long-term relationships helps us to understand some of the unconscious contributions to typical difficulties presented in couple therapy. In particular, he is helpful in illuminating how we dampen desire in our primary relationships by making the other person safe and predictable: 'This is why, for so many couples, sex becomes routinized and boring over time. It is not that familiarity breeds lack of interest, but that as mutual dependencies deepen, as shared lives become more complexly intertwined, sexual passion, with all its accompanying risks, becomes increasingly dangerous' (pp. 191—192).

Conclusion

Self-psychological and intersubjective approaches offer a rich understanding of the archaic needs that structure much conflict in couples. The concepts of selfobject experiences, selfobject transferences, and narcissistic vulnerability provide a clear map that assists the therapist to fully understand some of the dynamics lying underneath the surface of couple conflict. The techniques of empathic immersion, careful investigation, and legitimization of the underlying vulnerability of each partner's self and strengthening affect regulation are the core interventions in assisting distressed couples. These techniques are very similar to those utilized by Emotionally Focused Couple Therapy (EFCT), although the underlying mechanisms of change are somewhat different. Self psychology also offers a much fuller explanation and greater developmental understanding about why conflict and distress occur.

Attachment theory also adds an important dimension to the psychodynamics of couple relationships. It assists us to understand more about the developmental origins of attachment behaviour, the strategies individuals use in relationships, and the importance of developing reflective function in the couple. Although explanatory mechanisms are somewhat different, again there is a good deal of overlap between attachment theory and self psychology in terms of understanding the processes that lead to couple distress. We will return to the psychodynamics of the couple relationship in Chapters 5—8, where we will draw on these very helpful constructs to inform the practice of couple therapy.

3

Thinking Systemically About the Couple

Introduction

The couple relationship does not only exist in the mind of the two partners or in the intersubjective space between them. It also exists in the interpersonal interaction between the two partners, interaction which has an observable structure and process, and which influences and is influenced by the wider social system of which the couple is a part. To understand this interpersonal aspect of the couple relationship, we draw in particular upon the field of family therapy. Couple therapy, of course, is not synonymous with family therapy — it is not family therapy 'writ small', involving a 'simpler' system of only two people — any more than it is synonymous with individual therapy. However, the systemic thinking that has evolved within family therapy provides another necessary resource for understanding the intricacies of the couple relationship, as well as for understanding and helping individuals in their relational and social context (Hedges, 2005). In particular, systemic theory helps the couple therapist to locate the couple relationship within the wider social and cultural context, a context that is constantly changing and evolving (Gorrell-Barnes, 2004).

Some important family systems concepts

It is not possible in the space of a short chapter to summarize the whole of family systems thinking, and we will therefore concentrate on a few concepts that we have found to be particularly relevant to work with couples. More detailed accounts of the theory are readily available in a number of texts such as those by Dallos & Draper (2005), Nichols & Schwartz (2001), and Kogan & Gale (2000).

An interpersonal focus and circular causality

At the core of a systemic perspective on couple relationships is a focus on the interactive pattern that occurs between the partners, not on individual symptoms or pathology. This focus on interaction requires the therapist to be *observing patterns and sequences* rather than searching for or ascribing motives or causes. From a systemic perspective, no action in a relationship occurs in a vacuum: each is a response to the reaction, actual or anticipated, of the other, in a never-ending circle of recursive interaction. As Nichols & Schwartz (2001) comment,

> Linear cause and effect are lost in a circle of mutual causality. This idea of mutual or *circular causality* was useful for therapists because so many families expect to find the cause of their problems and determine who is responsible. Instead of joining the family in a logical but unproductive search for who started what, circular causality suggests that problems are sustained by an ongoing series of actions and reactions, and that you don't have to get back to first causes to change an interaction.
>
> (p. 108, italics in original)

Thus — as will be described in more detail in Chapter 6 — the couple therapist needs always to be focused not only on what one partner is currently saying, but also on looking for clues to the way the other is responding, and using those clues to open up the interactive pattern of the relationship for exploration.

Homeostasis and morphogenesis

When a system is perturbed at a change in one part, the system as a whole will be affected and will react to restore the previously existing balance. This tendency, to return to a 'steady state', is a property of systems known as 'homeostasis'. Understanding homeostasis can help the therapist to make sense of interactive patterns in the system, for example when an apparently helpful initiative by a family member sets in train a process of negative feedback in the family, leading to a return to a less satisfactory or symptomatic situation. It can also help the therapist in finding ways of increasing the perturbation in the system so that it cannot return to the original state of balance but has to find a new one — a process of morphogenesis, the family changing form (Dell, 1982). Morphogenesis is also an inherent feature of family systems, due to the physical and emotional maturing and changing of the individual family members who make up the family. Family systems thus alternate between stability and change, between homeostasis and morphogenesis. Sometimes the process of adaptation can become stuck in a family, and the therapist needs to find ways of stimulating the process of change so that the family system can resume its own development.

Sandie and Neville were in a second marriage. Sandie had lost her first husband in traumatic circumstances, whilst Neville had an emotionally deprived childhood, fell passionately in love and married at a young age, and had been deeply hurt when his young wife was soon unfaithful to him. Now in their mid-thirties, Sandie and Neville cared deeply about each other but their relationship seemed constantly to be threatened by conflicts over apparently insignificant issues, to the point where they wondered if they were 'incompatible'.

After some eight conjoint sessions, a breakthrough seemed to come when both were able to admit to their vulnerability and — more importantly — to their fear that the other would not be able to accept and respond to their vulnerability if it were more openly expressed. For Sandie, this seemed to revolve around 'unfinished business' about the trauma associated with her first husband's death, and for Neville there was a deeply held conviction that any relationship would only lead to hurt if he allowed himself to become too dependent on it. The therapist observed that their fights were a form of safety mechanism that was activated whenever they started to get too close or too dependent on each other. This seemed like an important session, but it was followed by a series of postponed appointments, each with an apparently valid excuse being given. Perhaps the therapy sessions had now become a place where the balance of their relationship would be threatened by too much vulnerability being expected?

Eventually Sandie arrived on her own for a joint session. The therapist proceeded with the session; Sandie said nothing had really changed, and then went on to talk about her awareness of a pattern of accommodating to the needs and expectations of others. She experienced that pattern with Neville, but especially with her elderly mother, who treated her protectively as if she were still a child in many ways. She thought that if she could learn to 'be her own person' more with her mother, that would make it easier for her in her relationship with Neville. The therapist suggested a strategy for gradually changing her part in the pattern of interaction with her mother — but warned her that the pressure from her mother to accommodate would almost certainly increase before the relationship eventually changed.

The 'breakthrough' session had been destabilizing for the system, and the missed sessions were another way of restoring a state of homeostasis in Sandie and Neville's relationship. At the same time, a process of morphogenesis had perhaps begun: Sandie had come to a session even though Neville found an excuse not to, and she wanted to address an issue that would doubtless create further pressure for change in the system of their relationship.

Communication and meta-communication

Communication is obviously a central and essential element of a couple's relationship. The pattern of communication a couple develop will be governed by rules about communication — implicit or explicit rules about what can and cannot be talked about, and about how things can be talked about. Sometimes, when there is a noticeable change in the tone of the session after the couple therapist asks a question, the therapist will sense that they are perhaps asking a couple to break a rule of their relationship about communication. Often the rule will exist to protect the couple from difficult emotions or from remembering painful experiences: Virginia Satir, one of family therapy's early pioneers, demonstrated this function of communication both in her books (1983; 1988) and in her powerful experiential workshops. Making explicit and thus open to discussion a couple's rules about communication is an important task of the couple therapist.

Communication between partners in a relationship is also 'punctuated' by the partners, as each makes assumptions about cause and responsibility. This is linear, cause-and-effect, thinking — John does X and Mary then does Y — which, in this example, ascribes primacy to John's action X. Circular causality, however, requires us to look at what comes before John's action X and after Mary's action Y; when we do so, we usually find a pattern where neither partner's behaviour has primacy. The classic, if simplistic, example is 'she drinks, he nags, she drinks, he nags' — is it the drinking that 'causes' the nagging, or the nagging that 'causes' the drinking? In couple therapy, it is a common pattern in the early stages of therapy for each partner to put a great deal of energy into trying to convince the therapist that the other partner is the one at fault. Thus, John says, 'if Mary would be responsible and didn't drink so much and embarrass me, I could relax and not be constantly checking on her when we are out enjoying ourselves at a social function', and Mary says, 'if I didn't feel so tense because of John constantly criticizing me I would feel more confident, and I don't think I would drink nearly so much'. The challenge for the therapist is to help the partners find different ways of punctuating their communication, with the aim of helping both to take responsibility for changing their own behaviour, rather than trying to change the other's behaviour.

Communication conveys information — facts, feelings, or perceptions — from one partner to the other. The same act of communication also conveys information about the relationship between the two partners, known as 'meta-communication'. If the couple therapist begins the first conjoint meeting with the couple with an invitation to say what has brought them to therapy, and if that invitation is addressed equally to both partners, there will often be some brief communication between the partners as to who begins. Mary may make the simple statement to John 'you go first', but that act of communication will contain a meta-communication. Those three words could indicate that Mary is deferring to John, or that she is ordering him to begin, or perhaps that she is punishing him ('you can explain why we are in such a mess in our marriage because of your misbehaviour') or is protecting him emotionally ('I know how distressed you are, your need is greatest, so you begin and get it off your chest'). The couple therapist needs to learn to hear the meta-communication as well as listen to the content of what is being said.

Subsystems and boundaries

In his classic text *Families and Family Therapy*, Salvador Minuchin (1974) describes a method for 'mapping' the family system — that is, for observing the processes of interaction and the structure of the system that gave rise to those processes, and then recording the system diagrammatically. Minuchin argues that whilst a family can have a variety of subsystems, there are three subsystems that are inherent in any two-generational family. These are the *spouse subsystem* (concerned with the meeting of the emotional and affiliative needs of the adult couple in the family), the *parental subsystem* (responsible for meeting the need for parenting of the children in the family, and for exercising age-appropriate authority), and the *sibling subsystem* (responsible for meeting the socialization needs of the children in the family). In a single-parent family there will need to be accommodation so that the functions of the spouse and parenting subsystems can still be met, and if there is only one child there will need to be accommodation so that the needs of the sibling subsystem can be met. Membership of each subsystem is not determined by age or gender, but by function. Thus, if one parent frequently works away from home for extended periods, a child in the family may be drawn into the spousal subsystem (as a confidant of the parent who is at home) or into the parenting subsystem (as an auxiliary parent or 'parenting child', helping to provide 'parenting' for younger siblings). Similarly, a parent may become a member of the sibling subsystem, colluding with the children against the other parent ('he/she is so irresponsible — it's as if I have an extra child to look after much of the time').

The boundaries between subsystems define who participates in the subsystem's activities and the way they participate. Boundaries are, Minuchin argues, are on a continuum from permeable (or diffuse) to impermeable (or rigid). Family systems characterized by a preponderance of very rigid boundaries have a 'disengaged' family structure — difficulty or stress for a family member does not carry over the subsystem boundary, and support is not forthcoming. If, however, the boundaries between family subsystems are predominantly diffuse, the family structure is what Minuchin terms 'enmeshed' — individual autonomy of family members is subordinated to family loyalty and belonging; if 'one family member sneezes, all family members catch their cold'. Whilst disengaged and enmeshed family structures are not in themselves a problem, they do over time tend to give rise to difficulties because they are inflexible and cannot cope with the inevitable changes that are required as family members grow and their needs change. By contrast, families that have 'clear' boundaries that are sufficiently open (permeable) to allow communication and engagement across the subsystem boundary, but sufficiently firm (impermeable) to allow a sense of separateness, individuality, and difference for family members, will be able to be more flexible and adaptable.

The couple therapist, although working only with the couple, will often need to work on issues to do with boundaries between family subsystems. For example, there may be a need to protect the spousal or parenting subsystems and clarify their boundaries by reducing the involvement of children or the parents of one or both partners. At other times, boundaries may need to be relaxed so that the appropriate functions can be included and exercised in a subsystem, for example by permitting nurturing of the partners by each other in the spousal subsystem or by allowing anger and limit setting in the parental subsystem.

Penny and Richard both had demanding professional positions, and earned good incomes, but were 'time poor' in terms of couple and family relationships. Penny took on much of the parenting, often leaving Richard feeling excluded; this had increased since the diagnosis of their teenage daughter, the eldest child, with bi-polar disorder. Penny felt obliged to do the best she could to help her daughter and worked heroically to support her, but also tried not to neglect the other two children. Richard thought Penny was over-involved as a parent, especially with their bi-polar daughter; he had become increasingly involved in the sporting activities of the other two children, wanting to compensate for the disruption caused by their sister's condition. He was the 'good' parent giving the children what they wanted; she was the 'bad' parent who often said 'no'. There was growing conflict between them about parenting, which precipitated their seeking therapy. They also had an extensive network of friends, with whom they tried to keep in touch. They rarely had private time to talk as a couple, and any social or leisure activity as a couple inevitably involved socializing with others.

There were developmental issues relating to family-of-origin experiences that needed to be worked on for both Penny and Richard, but part of what their therapist did was to 'clear the ground' for this work by seeking to clarify the subsystems and boundaries in the family. He sought to involve Richard more actively in the parental subsystem, whilst lessening his involvement in the sibling subsystem of the two younger children. At the same time, he encouraged Penny to allow Richard into the parenting subsystem by requesting his help instead of assuming that he would be too tired to assist her. He also helped them create clearer, less permeable, boundaries around their relationship as a couple, by making their bedroom a 'no-go area' for the children so that they had somewhere to talk privately, and also by encouraging them to say 'no' to some social engagements so that they could enjoy time out as a couple.

Circular questioning

In the conjoint session, a question is usually addressed to a partner or family member in a manner that requires that person to respond for themselves. If the person responds by talking about the feelings, needs, or motives of another family member, the therapist will often remind them to 'each speak for yourself'. There is a danger, however, that this encourages linear, cause-and-effect, thinking, rather than focusing attention on the interconnectedness and interdependence of the relationship system. The technique of circular questioning stems from the work of the Milan Associates (Cecchin, 1987), and aims at asking questions that focus on the circular nature of relationships. A circular question asks the person to whom the question is addressed to see themselves in a relational context and to see that context from the point of view of the other participant(s) in the relationship. Thus the therapist might ask, 'how would your husband's parents describe your husband's perception of your way of responding when you and he disagree about disciplining your children?' Circular questioning is not a 'technique' aimed at eliciting a particular response from the family member, but represents an orientation of curiosity about relationships that the therapist seeks to have characterize the conjoint session.

Externalizing the problem

The statement 'the person is not the problem' has become a catchcry of the narrative therapy of Michael White and his colleagues (White, 1989, 1995; White & Epston, 1990), directing our attention to the 'problem-saturated stories' of many seeking the help of a therapist. People's stories are 'problem saturated' in the sense that their experience of their problems has come to define who they are as a person; they cannot think of themselves without thinking of their problem. The therapist working in the narrative tradition seeks to ask questions that separate the person from the problem. Thus the person does not 'have' low self-esteem as if it were a part of them, an element of their identity as a person, but 'low self-esteem' is seen as a separate entity, external to them as a person, that leads them to think or act in certain ways. The therapist seeks to have the person name the problem — perhaps 'self-doubt' — and then asks questions that assume the problem is an entity external to the person: 'when your self-doubt is active, how does it persuade you to feel anxious?', 'when you want to express affection to your wife, how does self-doubt tell you to behave?', or 'how do you think self-doubt has been able to influence your relationship?' This, in turn, leads to exploration of when the problem has not been able to influence the person, to exceptions to the problem story, and to the question of who is in control, the person or the problem? Exploring exceptions also helps the couple to see that other interaction patterns exist and frees them from totalizing constructs such as 'he never listens to me' or 'she always undermines my discipline with the kids'. If alternatives to these behaviours have happened once, the couple therapist can work on amplifying the exceptions so that they happen again, more frequently.

When a relationship is in difficulty, the potential consequences can seem so enormous that the problem seems to dominate the partners' lives: they merge their identity with their problem. Finding ways of helping the partners to stand back and see themselves, their relationship, and their problem in perspective can be important, but difficult to accomplish. With some couples, an externalizing conversation provides an effective way to do this.

Bowen Theory

Murray Bowen was one of the seminal thinkers of the early family therapy movement, and his ideas have particular relevance for understanding the couple relationship within the family system. Bowen's family systems theory (later renamed 'Bowen Theory' to distinguish it from other systemic approaches) saw the family as an emotional unit, and had its roots not in general systems theory and cybernetics but in evolutionary biology. The family as an emotional system is energized by the 'interplay between two counterbalancing life forces — *individuality* and *togetherness*' (Kerr & Bowen, 1988, p. 59). The product of this interplay between the forces for individuality and togetherness is a patterning of relationships unique to the particular family, a relationship system where change in one part of the system leads to responses by other parts. Bowen developed eight interlocking concepts as the core of his theory, these eight concepts making up an integrated whole. We will look at three of his ideas that have proven particularly useful in work with couples: differentiation of the self, the role of the triangle in relationships, and the cross-generational patterning of relationships depicted in the genogram.

Differentiation of self

Bowen understood the newborn child to be in a state of fusion or symbiosis with the mother, incapable of separate existence: the togetherness force dominates. Mother and infant instinctively respond to each other, and initially there is no sense for the infant of being separate. The emergence of a sense of a separate self from this initial symbiotic state is one of the primary developmental tasks during the years of childhood and adolescence. By the time the stage of young adulthood is reached, the person has hopefully developed a capacity to be an individual in their own right. That is, they are able to know what is *their* experience and *their* position, rather than accommodating to or simply accepting the position of their parents, or, alternatively, having to defensively cut off from relationships with parents or family members. There is a balance between the force for togetherness and the force for independence. Bowen theory terms this process 'the differentiation of the self': it involves the child learning to separate from parents whilst still maintaining a connection, and at the same time being able to assert their independence by expressing their own thoughts and feelings which are different from those of their parents.

The process of differentiation of the self of the person is not an either/or matter — differentiated or not differentiated — but should be understood as being represented by a position on a continuum; thus Bowen theory talks of a *level of differentiation* with regard to the self. Central to the process of differentiation of self is the interplay between thinking and emotion — that is, the extent to which the person has developed a capacity for being aware of and thinking about their emotional experience, even in the face of anxiety; or, alternatively, the extent to which emotions dominate and 'crowd out' any capacity for self-awareness and reflection when anxiety rises. A person with a lower level of differentiation of self has difficulty distinguishing between thinking and feeling: they are therefore likely to be more emotionally reactive in relationships, especially when anxiety increases. By contrast, a person with a higher level of differentiation of self is able to discriminate between thinking and emotion — they are, in effect, able to *think about* their feelings, and thus are less emotionally reactive in their relationships.

For example, a person may say to their partner, 'I'm really hurt that you've forgotten my birthday', and their partner might respond with defensive anger — 'that's right, blame me, I can never do anything right where you are concerned. You just conveniently forget how busy I've been recently.' Such a response would suggest a lower level of differentiation of self: the partner feels something — perhaps guilt or shame at their failure — but is not able to allow themselves time to be aware of, to think about, that feeling, and to make a thoughtful choice about how they will respond. If they were able to respond from a point of greater differentiation, they might say something like 'Yes, I know you're upset, and I'm really sorry about that. I've been very preoccupied recently and it slipped my mind, but that isn't really any excuse. I'm feel quite embarrassed, and I would like to make it up to you in some way.'

Some critics (Luepnitz, 1988) have accused Bowen's concept of differentiation of self as privileging thought over emotion, male instrumentality over female expressiveness, and thus demonstrating the patriarchal views of his time and culture. It is important to note, however, that differentiation of self is about a capacity to *both* think *and* feel. The greater a person's level of differentiation, the greater capacity they will have to remain in touch with their emotional experience. Thus, their capacity is greater for engaging emotionally with others, and for staying engaged even when there is tension or anxiety in the relationship.

Differentiation of self is a process that is never completed. Whilst the basic pattern may be set by the time we reach early adulthood, later life experiences (including participation in counselling or psychotherapy) can enable further differentiation to occur. Conversely, under circumstances of stress or heightened anxiety, regression to a lower level of differentiation, to a more reactive position, can occur. To illustrate this, Bowen (Kerr & Bowen, 1988) talked in terms of a 'scale of differentiation of self' that went from '0' to '100'. It is important to realize that this scale, as Bowen conceived it, is intended as a visual aid or metaphor, *not* as an empirically tested psychometric scale — although attempts have been made to develop empirically validated instruments that measure aspects of the person's level of differentiation of self (Searight, 1997). Bowen's understanding was that nobody is at '0', the absolute bottom of the scale of differentiation, unless they are in a chronically psychotic state. Similarly, nobody is at '100', fully differentiated. The mid-point on the scale represents a beginning capacity to be aware of the difference between feelings and thoughts, and to make decisions about responses or action based on that awareness.

Two useful points follow from Bowen's idea of a person's level of differentiation of self. First, Bowen theory suggests that in the process of choosing a partner, people will tend to find a partner whose level of differentiation of self is similar to their own. An implication of this for couple therapy is that whilst one partner may initially present as the stronger or more emotionally intact partner and the other presents as more emotionally reactive or fragile, both will usually need to work on issues relating to their degree of differentiation of self.

Marcus was a successful professional man, busy and competent, and devoted to his family. He and Robyn presented for therapy seeking help for a pattern in their relationship whereby there would be frequent upsets over relatively minor incidents that would result in Robyn becoming first very angry and then hurt and withdrawn for a period of some days. Marcus would be long suffering and patient, and would usually be the one who initiated a reconciliation.

Marcus gave the impression of being a very reasonable man; he acknowledged that he was perhaps not easy to live with because he did like things done in an orderly way, and he was often tired in the evenings and weekends due to the professional demands placed on him. However, unless Robyn could learn to be less volatile, less emotional, in her outbursts of anger, and more able to discuss matters calmly, he did not know how much longer he could continue in the marriage. Robyn was well aware of her emotional volatility, which she saw as stemming from her chaotic childhood with an alcoholic father and a chronically depressed mother. She experienced Marcus, however, as being 'always right' and his set views as quite controlling.

Their initial story was that Robyn needed more help than Marcus. Robyn's emotional reactivity suggested that she had a lower level of differentiation of self than Marcus, and it would have been easy to focus the therapy on her — perhaps even to suggest that couple therapy was not appropriate and to refer her to individual therapy. As couple therapy developed, however, it became apparent that Marcus had as much difficulty in owning and communicating his emotional experience as Robyn did. Her reactivity took the form of angry outbursts; his took the form of a retreat into logic and reasonableness, behind which he became emotionally unavailable. Robyn started to make some progress in therapy, becoming less volatile and angry, and starting to seek more emotional intimacy with Marcus; and, perhaps not surprisingly, Marcus found it difficult to respond. He was then able to begin looking more at his own fear of emotion and his inability to recognize, own, and communicate his feelings.

Both Robyn and Marcus needed to be able to develop greater levels of differentiation of self. In Marcus' case, there was a well-developed *pseudo-self* — a way of being that is based on what others are perceived to find acceptable, rather than on a grounded, authentic sense of the individual's self (Kerr & Bowen, 1988). That worked well for Marcus much of the time in his professional relationships, but it failed him when anxiety increased in a more important and intimate relationship such as with Robyn.

A second important implication of the idea of differentiation of self concerns the therapeutic process. In general, the greater the therapist's level of differentiation of self, the more effective they are likely to be in assisting their clients to become more differentiated. Most therapists will know situations where they have reached the edge of their capacity to stay differentiated. This is the point at which they have either become reactive to the client, by getting angry or failing to maintain appropriate boundaries in some way, or by 'escaping' in an uncharacteristic way into problem-solving and advice-giving, or by feeling compelled to refer the client to someone else for reasons that do not withstand more considered scrutiny. Bowen theory indicates that it is important for the therapist to be able to maintain a differentiated stance whilst with the couple. This will involve not taking sides, not being pulled into being part of a triangle with them, and not reacting to the couple's emotionality. This will require an awareness of both the transference and the countertransference processes occurring in the session:

> The client's transference with the therapist is part of the togetherness force in the therapy relationship. The client may push the therapist to agree with him/her, seek the therapist's approval, ask for advice or direction, or become critical or angry with the clinician. . . . The other part of the clinical fusion is the therapist's countertransference, which may express itself in distance, yawning, falling asleep, forgetting an appointment, telling the client what to do, criticising the client, losing a sense of humour, seeking the client's approval or agreement, worrying about the client, or being too personal.
>
> The clinician's 'I position' [differentiated position] provides some separateness in the midst of the togetherness. The 'I position' is the clinician defining a self in words or actions with the client or staying connected yet detached.
>
> (Klever, 1998, p. 136, parentheses added)

It is therefore not surprising that Bowen emphasized personal work by the therapist as a key component of the psychotherapy training process, aimed at the therapist achieving a greater degree of differentiation from his or her own family of origin.

Triangles

Bowen did not invent or discover triangles; they are ubiquitous in human relationships, and in various ways earlier writers had described them before Bowen — including Freud, whose description of the Oedipal situation is essentially about the triangle between the young child, the mother, and the father (Freud, 1909). Bowen did, however, focus attention on the process by which triangles are formed and on the importance of resolving rigid triangles so that the family system could regain a degree of flexibility (Bowen, 1978; Kerr & Bowen, 1988).

The stability of a two-person relationship will depend on two factors, the level of differentiation of the two parties to the relationship, and the degree of anxiety involved in their relationship. When there is an increase in anxiety in a relationship, resulting in an increased level of stress, there will come a point at which the level of differentiation of the two parties is insufficient to manage the degree of stress involved, and a third party is 'triangled in' to reduce the tension. Building on Bowen's work, Fogarty (1979) talks of 'movement' in relationships that is part of the management of closeness and distance, with each partner moving towards or away from the other, both emotionally and literally. Triangles are formed as a result of this movement, becoming 'a short-circuiting mechanism that serves the purpose of avoiding discomfort with intimacy and of avoiding discomfort with facing conflictual issues' (Guerin, Fogarty, Fay & Kautto, 1996, p. 13). A parent might, for example, move towards a child seeking closeness in order to manage a sense of aloneness and distance in their relationship with their spouse.

Couple therapists who follow Bowen theory will view all marriages as involving a process of triangulation, with the intensity of the process depending on the level of differentiation that the partners have been able to achieve with their family of origin (Klever, 1998). Thus, an important part of the assessment process is identifying the interlocking pattern of triangles occurring in the family system. The triangles that the couple therapist may need to attend to will be both within the current family, between parents and child/children, and also across the generations, involving one or both partners and their parent(s) and/or sibling(s).

Pam and Steven's 23-year relationship had always been volatile. Both came from highly dysfunctional families of origin; a shared fear of intimacy, balanced with an equally strong fear of abandonment, led to them relating in a highly reactive style. Couple therapy was triggered by a number of painful and unresolved arguments following an anxious time of career change for Steven. They initially responded well to couple therapy and appeared highly motivated to improve their relationship. They recognized that as their late-teenage children were starting to lead more independent lives, they wanted more fulfilment from their relationship as a couple.

After a few sessions, it seemed that Pam and Steven were making good use of the opportunity afforded by therapy, and were beginning to be a little less reactive towards each other. Both reported feeling more relaxed and more able to let their guard down with each other, they were talking more intimately than they had for a long time, and they began to enjoy their sexual relationship in a way that had not been possible for some years. Conflict, however, then began to re-emerge in their relationship, focused on a series of triangles in their wider family system. One triangle involved Pam complaining bitterly about Steven constantly siding with their 19-year-old daughter, whom she perceived as failing to treat her with respect. Another triangle involved Steven feeling trapped and resentful by Pam's refusal to welcome his sister as a visitor to their home, and angry that Pam often criticized his sister when talking to him, but refused to speak directly with his sister about the behaviour that annoyed her. Neither of these conflicts were new: they both seemed to be triangles that had existed for many years, and which were reactivated from time to time.

Pam and Steven had initially responded to the therapy by moving closer together, but as they did so, their anxiety about being intimate increased; familiar triangles were then called into play, providing a focus for their anxiety and restoring distance in their relationship as a couple.

It is important to keep in mind that a threesome is not necessarily a triangle; it becomes one when there is a degree of reactivity in the relationship between the three parties that controls behaviour. The key to working with triangles is to redirect the 'movement' in the triangle so that the symptomatic behaviour represented by the triangle becomes redundant. Guerin and his colleagues describe the process as creating 'an experiment' that requires one or more members of the family system to move in a direction opposite to that determined by the emotion and reactivity within their relationship (Guerin et al., 1996). Thus, with Pam and Steve, the therapist experienced considerable 'pull' towards becoming a mediator in the triangles involving Pam and Steve's daughter and Steve's sister. However, recognizing the triangles enabled the therapist to maintain the focus on the heightened anxiety in Pam and Steve's relationship; he structured ways in which they could experiment with remaining in closer emotional contact with each other, even though their anxiety initially increased as they did so.

The multigenerational family system: Utilizing the genogram

As with the concept of the triangle, Bowen did not discover the impact that family relationship experiences in the family of origin have on the emotional and psychological functioning of the person in the present. He did, however, demonstrate more clearly than had been done before how patterns of relating in the family emotional process are transmitted from one generation to another. He also went on to show how understanding and intervening in this cross-generational process is often an important element in making it possible for relationship patterns in the present to change. Whilst Bowen clearly saw the focus of therapy as being on relationship difficulties in the present, he also viewed the process of understanding the inherited cross-generational pattern of family dynamics as being an important key for unlocking relationship difficulties in the present.

Bowen's term for this cross-generational dimension of family functioning is 'the multigenerational family projection process'. Bowen theory suggests that the level of differentiation of John and Mary in their couple relationship will, to a significant extent, be a consequence of the degree of anxiety projected onto them by their parents in their family of origin.

For example, John may have had a father who lacked self-confidence and who coped with that lack of confidence by projecting his anxiety and self-doubt onto John — who was then treated as if he needed protection. This might well create a self-fulfilling prophecy, whereby John grows up either with poor self-esteem and lacking confidence, or with an overly confident persona developed as a cover for his doubts about himself. Either solution will effect John's own sense of self, and thus his functioning both as a husband to Mary and as a parent to their children.

Imagine now that Peter, one of John and Mary's children, seeks help as an adult, wanting to understand and change some difficulties in the way in which he functions in his own relationship with a partner. For the therapist to help Peter to understand the relationship dynamics back into his grandparents' generation — that is, to understand how his father John was over-protected by his grandfather and how that impacted on John and on John's functioning as a husband and father — will make it easier for Peter to free himself from his family's multigenerational pattern of relating.

Bowen went a step further, however. From his pioneering experience in seeking to understand and change his own family system, he came to believe that for the adult to actually 'go home again' (Framo, 1976, 1992; McGoldrick, 1995) and find ways of engaging differently with their family of origin could become a pivotal point for change.

> Sean was a successful business executive. Married with grown-up children, he was aware that his marriage of some 34 years was emotionally empty and sterile. He put more and more effort into work to avoid having to be home with his wife. He had an extended affair with a woman he came to love, and with whom he found a previously unknown level of emotional fulfilment. But — he could not leave his wife. Every time he tried to separate, she would become angry and upset, and he could not do it. Yet — as soon as the emotional storm had passed, he would kick himself for not having had the courage to leave, which he knew for a certainty was what he wanted to do. Several attempts at therapy got nowhere.
>
> Eventually, in individual therapy, Sean gradually came to recognize the way in which the pattern of his relationship with his wife mirrored the pattern of his relationship with his mother — an emotionally needy woman who controlled him when he was young by her threats of getting upset if he went against her wishes. Even now, as an adult, he easily slipped into the pattern of being responsible for his mother's emotional well-being and for not upsetting her. For example, when on a business trip with a demanding schedule he would go out of his way to visit his mother; but if he was the slightest bit late arriving, she would be upset and criticize him, and he would feel guilty for letting her down. Even the prospect of arriving late at his mother's home would cause him anxiety. As he understood this pattern, he began the process of engaging differently with his mother, starting to have a sense of his own adult authority in his family-of-origin system (Williamson, 1991). Before long, he was eventually able to follow through with the process of separating from his wife.

To enable the therapist to document the complexity of family membership across three or more generations, and — more importantly — to record the nature of the dyadic relationships, the triangles, and the movement within the triangles, across the generations, Bowen developed the multigenerational genogram (Bowen, 1978; McGoldrick, Gerson, & Shellenberger, 1999). Developed in a collaborative process with the client or with the couple during the assessment phase of therapy, the genogram becomes a map for the ensuing therapy process. Often the process of constructing the genogram, although part of the assessment stage of the therapy, proves to be a powerful intervention in its own right. Thinking about the relationships depicted in the genogram sometimes leads to memories being triggered, either at the time of constructing the genogram or later, and the experiences associated with those memories can open fruitful avenues for exploration as the therapy proceeds.

Relationship systems across time

One of the enduring ideas to come from family systems theory concerns the way relationships within the family system change over time (Carter & McGoldrick, 2005; Gerson, 1995). This process of change is usually described as a developmental process, with each phase building on the changes negotiated in earlier phases. Seeing the family as developing across time in this way is not a new idea; many frameworks, based on research or on clinical experience with families, have been put forward (Gerson, 1995). William Shakespeare's 'seven ages of man' depicted in *As You Like It* (Wells & Taylor, 1987) is often quoted, with its eloquently described progression from 'infant, mewling and puking in the nurse's arms', through to 'the lover, sighing like a furnace', and on to an old age of 'second childishness and mere oblivion, sans teeth, sans eyes, sans taste, sans everything'. Similarly, we cannot help but be aware of a debt to Freud's seminal work on the development of the child, within the child's family context, through oral, anal, phallic, Oedipal, and latency phases (Waddell, 2002). The particular contribution of family systems theory has been to focus not just on the development of the individual within the family context, but on the ways in which the structure and dynamics *of the family itself* change over time.

Recognizing the stage of development that a particular family system has reached provides pointers to some of the issues that the family is likely to be facing in its ongoing developmental process. It also suggests ways in which the family may be struggling with residual issues that were not adequately resolved as it moved through earlier phases. However, thinking about the development of the family system over time requires that caution be exercised.

First, the family system is an abstraction, and its definition and boundaries are not fixed; each family system is also a subsystem of another family system. For example, a couple might be seen as having reached the stage where their children have left home and they themselves are entering a later stage of their family life cycle. That same couple, however, will occupy a different position if viewed from the vantage point of their elderly parents, and a different position again if viewed from the vantage point of one of their children who has committed to a partner and is expecting their first child. It is therefore important to keep in mind the complexity of each family unit as it reacts to past, present, and anticipated future relationships within the larger three-generational family system (Carter & McGoldrick, 2005).

Second, the impact of culture and of the wider social system will determine not only where the boundaries of the immediate family system are drawn, but also the ways in which stages of the family life cycle are lived out. Sometimes the impact of culture is gradual and near universal. One example of this in the Western world is the gradual but pronounced emergence of adolescence as a prolonged, socially recognized, and economically significant stage of development during the latter part of the twentieth century (Carter & McGoldrick, 2005). Similarly, changes in the role of women in both the community and within the family over recent decades have had a pronounced impact on the way various stages of the family life cycle are structured and on the experience of both women and men in those stages. Other influences on the ways in which stages of the family life cycle are lived out are more specific to a particular social or cultural context (McGoldrick, Giordano, & Garcia-Preto, 2005).

The family life cycle

The family life cycle is presented, in a simple six-stage format, in Table 3.1. The six stages fall into three groups, each with a different focus: forming the family system, expanding the family system, and contracting the family system. In each stage, there will be two types of changes the family system will need to negotiate:

- *First-order changes* are the practical and emotional adjustments the family and its members will need to make in order to meet the demands of that stage of the life cycle.
- *Second-order changes* are the changes that will need to made in the underlying patterning of relationships in the family system if the family is to adapt to a new stage of the family life cycle.

Table 3.1 The stages of the family life cycle

Focus*	Family life cycle stage*	First order changes	Second order changes
Partnering: Forming the system	1. The single young adult	■ Achieving financial independence. ■ Establishing adult identity. ■ Partner choice.	■ Differentiation of self from the family of origin.
	2. The committed couple	■ Establishing commitment. ■ Setting up a home and negotiating roles and lifestyle issues. ■ Negotiating differences.	■ Renegotiating relationships with the family of origin, with a shift of priority to the new 'family of orientation'. ■ Negotiating the 'rules about who makes the rules' (Haley, 1963).
The expanding system	3. The family with young children	■ Accommodating to the arrival of the first child: changes in work and financial arrangements, changes in organization of the home. ■ Negotiation of parental roles and responsibilities. ■ Practical and emotional tasks in adapting to, and coping with, the arrival of the second child and subsequent children.	■ Negotiating the move from a two-person to a three-person relationship system; issues of inclusion/exclusion, re-awakening of Oedipal issues, etc. ■ Negotiation of relationship with families of origin about roles of grandparents.
	4. The family with adolescents	■ Adapting to the expectations of greater independence of adolescents.	■ Accepting that parents are now 'on notice' of not being needed for parenting in the same way, and

(Continued)

Table 3.1 *(Continued)*

The contracting system	5. The couple with young adult children	■ Negotiation of more flexible family rules. ■ Adjusting to lesser involvement of adolescent children in family activities. ■ Financial stress of supporting adolescents as they move away from home into higher education or work. ■ Adjusting to greater freedom without focus on caring for children or adolescents. ■ Greater financial resources available. ■ Reassessing interests and focus of energy – on work, holidays, leisure interests, etc. ■ Incorporating new role of grandparent.	■ beginning to reduce investment of energy in parenting. ■ Re-evaluation of couple's sexual relationship as adolescents/young adults become sexually active and move into overtly sexual relationships. ■ Re-evaluation of couple relationship as primary relationship. ■ Renegotiation of issues of sharing of time, interests, and intimacy.
	6. The couple in later life	■ Adapting to retirement from workforce – lifestyle, health, financial issues.	■ Renegotiation of use of time, separately and as a couple. ■ Adapting to the need for support.

*Adapted from Gerson (1995)

The first-order changes are more widely recognized in the broader culture, and a store of cultural knowledge is available to family members facing these changes, not least from the popular media. However, the second-order changes are less obvious and are therefore less easily recognized as they occur. In many cases second-order changes will occur relatively easily and will hardly be noticed by family members. However, where there is difficulty in managing the transition into and through a new stage in the life cycle, the difficulty will more often lie in the domain of second-order change than that of first-order change.

The stages of the family life cycle described in Table 3.1 might be termed an 'ideal type'. In reality, allowance must be made for the impact of the larger social and cultural system on the issues relating to each stage, and on how these issues are perceived and responded to by a particular family. In addition, it is important to consider the particular circumstances of the family — including the family's ethnic tradition, any specific and idiosyncratic experiences, especially if traumatic, and structural changes or variations such as separation and divorce, being a single-parent family, and remarriage (Carter & McGoldrick, 2005; McGoldrick, 2002). Despite these caveats, however, the concept of the family life cycle provides a helpful starting point — a preliminary sketch map — for hypothesizing about the issues a couple may be facing at a particular stage of their family development and about ways in which these issues may be contributing to difficulties experienced in the couple's relationship.

The changing relationship of the couple

Another perspective on change in the couple relationship over time is given by looking at the changing emotional focus of the relationship as the couple move through the life cycle. Bader and Pearson provide such a framework in their text *In Quest of the Mythical Mate* (1988). Arguing that romantic love does not last forever, they seek to answer the question 'what do we do after we fall in love?' To provide an answer, they use as a metaphor Margaret Mahler's description of the process of early childhood development, a process that culminates in the 'psychological birth' of the human infant (Mahler, Pine, & Bergman, 1975).

Mahler described the relationship between child and mother as moving from a 'normal autistic' phase (from birth to 2 months) to a symbiotic phase (2—5 months), and then into an individuation/separation phase with the four sub-phases of differentiation (6—9 months), practising (10—16 months), rapprochement (17—24 months), and consolidation of individuality (after 24 months). Thus, by the age of 24 months, the child has 'a sense of individuality and an ability to form emotional connections that will endure the strains of real-life imperfections and absences' (Bader & Pearson, 1988, p. 8).

Bader and Pearson argue that the couple relationship develops through a sequence of stages that 'parallel the stages of early child-hood development described by Mahler' (p. 3). These stages are developmental, meaning that stages must be moved through pro-gressively with no stage skipped over, each stage being more com-plex than the preceding one, and that each stage provides the base for the next stage. Each stage involves specific tasks for the couple to master and involves a transformation of the couple relationship. Couples will not move neatly through the stages, and there will at times be regression to behaviour typical of the previous stage. Whilst one partner will usually move on to addressing the issues of the next phase before the other partner, conflict in relationships occurs when one or both partners become stuck in a stage of development and are unable to move on.

A brief description of the stages is as follows:

- *The symbiotic stage*: This involves the intensity of 'falling in love', with a desire to merge lives and to bond, and to overlook or minimize differences; there is a high level of mutual nurturing, of giving and receiving attention and affection, and of feeling special to the other; the relationship is exciting and stimulating, and a solid base of attachment is formed between the partners from which they can move on to explore difference.
- *The differentiation stage*: The partners start to see each other more realistically and start to recognise and face the differences as well as the similarities between themselves as people; they start to re-establish their own boundaries and to have separate as well as shared interests; they learn to face and resolve conflict. Sometimes the move into the differentiation stage for the couple is dramatic, precipitated by what feels like a disastrous fight, and sometimes it is more gradual and hardly noticeable — but the process is occur-ring nonetheless.
- *The practising stage*: Each partner now participates more in activities and relationships that separate them from each other; they are not so empathically attuned to each other, and they are more oriented to the external world; autonomy and individuality are important as they rediscover themselves as individuals and their place in the

world; conflicts become more intense, and they must learn to resolve conflicts so that they can maintain their emotional connection.

- *Rapprochement*: Having established a more solid sense of their individual identity in the world, the partners now look to each other for more intimacy; allowing vulnerability to be seen and responded to by the other becomes more important; there is a balance between 'we' and 'me'; periods of intimacy alternate with periods of re-establishing independence, but without arousing so much anxiety as would have been the case earlier in the relationship. There is less intensity, less sense of neediness, and a greater sense of choice about intimacy in the relationship.
- *Mutual interdependence*: 'two well-integrated individuals have found satisfaction in their own lives, have developed a bond that is deep and mutually satisfying, and have built a relationship based on a foundation of growth rather than on one of need' (Bader & Pearson, 1988).

As already indicated, each couple will have their own unique journey through these stages, influenced by both their own life experience and the larger context within which their relationship exists. Bader & Pearson (1988) suggest six common patterns amongst couples where the two partners are in different stages; this 'produces a "see-saw" effect in which the alternating pattern of conflict and withdrawal becomes dominant and is often experienced as impossible to change' (p. 14). At other times, 'both partners have remained in one stage too long and are finding it destructive' (p. 14). We would like to focus on two of these patterns which can create confusing difficulties for the therapist, namely two aspects of the situation where both partners are stuck in the symbiotic position:

- symbiotic/symbiotic, enmeshed
- symbiotic/symbiotic, hostile-dependent

For both types of symbiotic/symbiotic relationship, the underlying theme is the same — a fear of abandonment and a need to keep the other partner nearby. A couple where both partners are stuck in the symbiotic—symbiotic enmeshed pattern will be a couple who cannot allow awareness of any difference, let alone conflict, between them. There will be a sense of merging of experience such that the partners experience themselves as a 'we' rather than as two separate 'I's'; their language and non-verbal behaviour will communicate this. Such couples rarely seek couple therapy, although as time passes their children may begin to act out a sense of being engulfed by the enmeshing family system, either through exhibiting psychosomatic symptoms or by delinquent behaviour.

The symbiotic/symbiotic couple with a hostile-dependent pattern will present as having an exceptionally volatile relationship — 'their voices and body movements communicate ongoing anger, bitterness, and blame' (Bader & Pearson, 1988, p. 79) — engaging in repeated reactive fights, yet unable to separate. Beneath the fighting — often vitriolic — of such a couple lies both a *yearning for* and a *fear of* nurturing and intimacy, so that any move, by either partner, into either intimacy or separateness is experienced by the other partner as a threat that is reacted to with rage.

> The pattern is one … in which contradictory expectations and beliefs coexist. On the one hand, each believes the partner should provide total nurturance; on the other hand, each believes he or she does not deserve to receive such nurturance. So, ironically, partners expect nurturance, demand nurturance, yet also push it away when it is offered.
>
> (p. 80)

Such couples frequently present for couple therapy, and can easily defeat the efforts of the therapist who does not understand something of the underlying dynamics of their relationship system. Working with such couples first involves making the therapy space a safe environment for the couple by containing the conflict and the strong affect. The therapist must then find ways of enabling the partners to begin to

> see a larger picture, and, in doing so, to see and begin to accept the emerging self of the other. Helping the couple accomplish this rests on the building block of empathy.
>
> (Bader & Pearson, 1988, p. 96)

Conclusion

The couple relationship involves two individual partners and the relationship that has developed between them. The relationship will in part be a product of the internal world of each of the two partners, and, as shown in the previous two chapters, psychoanalytic theory is particularly useful in understanding this dimension of their relationship. The relationship will also be apparent in the structure and the patterning of the interaction between the two partners, and a range of theories that fall under the broad heading of 'family systems thinking' can be of use in illuminating this dimension of their relationship. In this chapter we have provided a brief overview of some important family systems concepts, with a particular focus on the work of Murray Bowen. We have also described theories that attempt to describe the changing pattern of the couple relationship over time, both in terms of the larger family system and in terms of the dynamics of the emotional relationship between the two partners.

4

But What About Love?

Introduction

Love, passion, sexuality, bonding, and commitment — how do these profound human experiences fit together? In the introduction to a book about a psychoanalytic perspective on love, Kernberg (1995) comments that whilst the subject of love has received attention over many centuries from philosophers and poets, and in more recent decades from sociologists and psychologists, 'surprisingly little about love can be found in the psychoanalytic literature'. We might add that there is even less attention given to love in the literature of family systems theory! Johnson (2004) makes a similar point: 'If we ask our clients what is the basis of a happy long-term relationship, they inevitably answer with one word, love. However, in the field of professional couple and family therapy, love has been conspicuous by its absence' (p. 24).

But — what does love in a committed relationship look like once the initial romantic excitement begins to subside? Writing from a psychoanalytic perspective, Person talks of affectionate bonding — 'based on mutuality and warmth, and, above all, on trust and loyalty' (Person, 1989), a state evocatively captured by Lasch's phrase 'haven in a heartless world' (Lasch, 1977). The relationship between the passion of falling in love and the achievement of a long-term affectionate bonding is complex. Person suggests that

> Affectionate bonding may be what is left of a love affair after the passionate component fades, but it may also have a life of its own in a relationship that was never passionate, never had any moments of transcendence, but always provided the kind of warmth and affection, tenderness, and nurturance that bind people together.
> (p. 325)

She also points out that 'affectionate bonding is often combined with sexuality, and this constitutes a very happy outcome for many lovers'.

In Woody Allen's movie Radio Days, set in the days of World War II, there is an early scene in which the tiny old grandfather is standing behind his more-than-buxom wife, trying to stuff her into one of the full-torso corsets women wore in the 1940s. The scene is comic, but it transcends the merely humorous, evoking as it does the casual yet tender earthiness of a couple who have shared half a century of physical intimacy. The two are at ease, deeply unashamed with one another despite the ravages of time and gravity, and their intimacy is extremely moving to the viewer.

(p. 327)

The couple therapist cannot ignore love or sexual experience, with the strong affects involved, of longing, eroticism and desire, loss and pain, betrayal, hatred, and despair. In this chapter we will look first at some recent ways in which emotions have been brought more into focus in understanding the couple relationship, and then at the issue of sexuality.

Emotion in the couple relationship

Emotionally Focused Couple Therapy

The EFCT model of therapy, initially developed by Greenberg & Johnson (1988) and further developed by Johnson (2004), has attracted a great deal of attention in recent years. Reasons for EFCT's popularity include the fact that it is a framework for brief therapy with couples and that it is structured in a way that makes it relatively easy to learn — although that does not necessarily equate with it being easy to use well in clinical practice. It is a model of therapy that has lent itself to empirical evaluation, and is now claimed to be the best validated form of couple therapy (Johnson, 2003). The EFCT website (www.eft.ca) claims that 70—75% of couples 'move from distress to recovery' and that 'approximately 90% show significant improvements'.

As well as drawing on earlier work on the processing of emotion in psychotherapy (Gendlin, 1981; Rice & Greenberg, 1984), EFCT utilizes attachment theory and systems theory to explain the repetitive cycles of emotional conflict that characterize distressed couple relationships. Attachment theory, and particularly adult attachment theory (Johnson & Whiffen, 2003; Shaver & Hazen, 1988), describes the forming of the strong emotional bond with a partner, who becomes a primary attachment figure. When this attachment bond is under threat or disrupted, emotional distress results. Systems theory is seen as providing not only the context of the couple relationship, but also a framework for understanding the pattern of interaction and the circular causality operating in the relationship — 'the pull of each partner's behaviour on the other' (Johnson, 2004, p. 48).

The EFCT model focuses on the basic emotional responses of anger, fear, surprise, joy, embarrassment/shame, disgust, hurt, sadness/despair. When the attachment bond is threatened or disrupted, there will be a primary emotional response — often fear or sadness. This primary emotional response is usually replaced, quickly, by a secondary emotional response that is defensive or adaptive in its function and aimed at getting the partner 'back into line'. It functions to remove the threat to the attachment bond. However, secondary emotional responses often elicit the opposite reaction from the partner to the one that is desired. For example,

- John feels fearful (primary emotional response) because he senses that Mary no longer loves him.
- His fear, a vulnerable emotion that he is not comfortable owning or allowing Mary to see, is quickly replaced by the secondary emotion of anger and he becomes critical of Mary's behaviour.
- Mary is hurt (primary emotional response) by John's accusations, but the hurt (too vulnerable an emotion to own and let John know about when he is angry) is quickly replaced by the secondary emotion of anger, and she counter-attacks indignantly.

It is these secondary emotions that become part of the repetitive interactional cycle, resulting in the ongoing distress or conflict that brings the couple to therapy. The therapeutic process in EFCT (described briefly in Chapter 7) is aimed at creating a safe environment in the therapy for the gradual 'unfolding' of the secondary emotional responses of the partners so that the primary emotional responses can be identified, owned, and expressed by the partners to each other — leading, hopefully, to a renewal and strengthening of the attachment bond.

The EFCT model is a major and significant development in couple therapy, not least because of its emphasis on working with the here-and-now emotional experience of the partners. However, as we have argued elsewhere (Crawley & Grant, 2005), EFCT fails to build on the psychodynamic nature of attachment theory. This results in an under-emphasis on the importance of exploring the relationship experience of the two partners in their families of origin, and insufficient attention being paid to the 'internal working model' of each partner and to the consequent way in which transference issues will play out in the therapeutic relationship. Recognizing the importance of family-of-origin experience and working through difficult legacies it may have left will also assist each partner in expanding their capacity for reflection as they seek to create a more coherent narrative about themselves, their histories, and their relationships with others.

The 'sound marital house' — the research of John Gottman

The research of John Gottman and his colleagues (Gottman, 1994a,b), together with the application of ideas about intervention with couples flowing from that research (Gottman, 1999, 2004; Gottman, Driver, & Tabares, 2002), comes from a very different theoretical base than the material presented so far in this book. Gottman is concerned with developing an empirical-based understanding of marriage relationships, including those factors that make for long-term success or for separation and divorce. Perhaps not surprisingly, his research suggests that emotions and how they are managed within the relationship are of central importance.

A starting point for Gottman is the original general systems theory of von Bertalanffy (1969), which Gottman describes as a 'dream (that) never became a reality' (Gottman et al., 2002, p. 390) due to its failure to provide an empirical base on which theory could be built. This has left the theory of family and couple therapy to operate at the level of hypothesis and assumption, rather than being refined and developed in a systematic manner. Gottman has set out to provide the empirical data that can support a theory of marital interaction, describing in quantitative terms and through mathematical modelling the processes by which a positive or a negative state of homeostasis is established and maintained in a marriage. This programme of research has used multi-method studies of couples, drawing upon data from observation of interactive behaviour, self-reports of experience, and measurement of levels of physiological arousal. The research has involved 7 longitudinal studies of over 667 couples, representative of 'stable and relatively happy marriages' ranging from the newly married through couples at the retirement end of the life span. It seeks to develop predictions as to which relationships will survive and which will end in divorce. It is not possible to do justice to Gottman's research in a brief overview, but a summary can be found in Gottman et al. (2002), and more extensive discussion in Gottman (1994a,b), and Gottman, Katz, & Hooven, (1996). More recently, Gottman has been concerned with developing ways of applying his research findings in interventive programmes, both through psycho-educational workshops for couples and through an approach to therapy entitled 'Gottman Method Couple Therapy' (Gottman, 1999; 2004).

Gottman's 'sound marital house' theory is central to both the research and the clinical work that Gottman undertakes, and a brief outline follows. The theory describes 'seven stories' of the marital house, the first three being the 'foundation' of the house.

- *Love maps* involve the partners' intimate knowledge of each other's internal world — likes, dislikes, history, values, and so on; how well do the couple know each other, and how up to date is that knowledge?
- *Fondness and admiration* involves the expression of feelings of care and respect by the partners for each other. Does this happen, or is it overlooked — with the consequence that partners feel lonely, uncared for?
- *Turning towards versus turning away* involves behaviours which seek connection and the balance between responding to such behaviours, ignoring them, or turning against them in everyday interaction.
- *Positive sentiment override* grows out of a solid foundation in the first three stories of the marital house, and describes the overall emotional ambiance of the relationship, where a neutral statement can be responded to positively. An example is given (Gottman, 2004) of one partner making a neutral statement such as 'You left the fan on in the bathroom again', with the other partner responding positively, 'Oh, right, I'll go and switch it off'. Alternatively, if negative sentiment override is in place, the response will be negative: 'Stop trying to control me, as if you never leave anything on.' The presence of positive sentiment override in the relationship is regarded as an important element in the couple's capacity to resolve problems.
- *Managing solvable problems*, the fifth story of the marital house, involves the skills of solving problems effectively. Gottman's

research indicates that only 31% of problems are solvable, the rest being 'perpetual problems' to do with lifestyle and personality. Solvable problems require the use of specific skills that can be learnt — the 'soft start-up' (stating the problem in a way that is non-accusatory and expresses need), 'repair' (bringing the conversation back on track if conflict starts to escalate), 'self-soothing' (taking a break, modulating arousal), accepting influence (acknowledging the validity of the other's position and negotiating change without giving up the core of one's own position), and 'compromise' (seeking to honour the each other's core needs).

- *Making dreams and aspirations come true* involves dialogue in which each partner attempts to appreciate the other's position over issues that present as perpetual problems to which there is no easy solution. Gottman describes the 'dream-within-conflict intervention' based on an assumption that often gridlocked conflicts involve underlying values and ideals that are not expressed.

- *Creating shared meaning* involves the couple exploring the beliefs they each have about philosophical or existential issues — what it means to each of them to be a parent, their spiritual beliefs, their aspirations, and so on. This final story of the house leads back to the first — that is, to a deepening and enriching of the love map each partner has of the other.

Therefore, presence of unresolvable problems in a couple's relationship is not the crucial issue. Rather, it is the affect that accompanies the unresolved problem that causes distress for couples; 'the goal is to establish a dialogue with a perpetual problem that communicates acceptance of the partner, and even amusement...' (Gottman et al., 2002, p. 379). The alternative is a gridlock situation, with the possible appearance of behaviour antithetical to the building of the sound marital house, the 'four horsemen of the apocalypse' — criticism, contempt, defensiveness, and stonewalling — which Gottman's research indicates to be predictive of marital failure.

The interventions Gottman and his colleagues have devised are presented in a behavioural format that at first sight does not sit comfortably with a psychodynamic orientation to couple therapy. The insights derived from Gottman's research are, however, worthy of careful consideration; in some instances at least, they can be seen as congruent with some of the ways in which psychodynamically oriented couple therapists think about relationships and the process of change (Sawyer, 2004).

Sexuality and couple therapy

Sometimes couples will seek therapy because they are aware of difficulties in their sexual relationship and wish to work on them. More often, however, the presentation will be couched in terms of some other relationship difficulty; the couple may or may not be aware of the importance of an underlying sexual difficulty.

Bert and Sally sought help because their marriage of five years' duration seemed to be deteriorating rapidly. They were growing apart, and experiencing frequent rows over trivial matters. The trouble had started after the birth of their first child. Bert was aware of Sally's preoccupation and unhappiness; he thought she was suffering from post-natal depression, which he had heard about. He was scared to confront her about his dissatisfaction with the relationship in case it made things worse for her, and 'bottled up' his feelings. He came from a family where negative feelings, especially anger, were never expressed.

Sally was not depressed in a clinical sense; but she herself was adopted as a baby, and her childhood in her adoptive family had been difficult, especially her relationship with her mother. Although presenting as a competent and confident 'can do' woman, she was in fact highly questioning of herself. The experience of becoming a mother had reawakened many doubts about her sense of self, including her sexual self-image.

Both regarded the virtual cessation of their sexual relationship as 'only to be expected' in the circumstances; they had not really talked about it, and did not mention it until asked by the therapist. Yet focusing on the dynamics of their sexual relationship proved to be a rapid and fruitful way of addressing the self-doubts and inhibitions that had put their relationship in peril.

Human sexuality is a multifaceted phenomenon, involving psychological, emotional, biological, relational, and cultural elements, and the expression of sexuality — or, in some instances, its lack of expression — is an important aspect of any committed couple relationship. It is therefore important that the couple therapist has an understanding of male and female sexual functioning, of the nature of sexual difficulties, and of the interrelationship between couple dynamics and sexuality.

Since the pioneering research of Masters and Johnson in the 1960s (Masters & Johnson, 1970), sex therapy has been available as a source of help for couples struggling with sexual dysfunction. The relationship between couple therapy and sex therapy has, however, not always been clear. Some couple therapists, finding it uncomfortable to talk about the specifics of a couple's sexual experience and practice, have tended to make the unwarranted assumption that if the quality of the couple's relationship improves, then their sexual difficulties will some-how 'automatically' be resolved. Conversely, the practitioner specializing in sex therapy may sometimes focus specifically on intervention into an aspect of sexual dysfunction but ignore the relational difficulties that provide the context of the sexual dysfunction. There has also been a tendency amongst couple therapists to focus on the consequences of sexual trauma, but to ignore what might be called 'everyday marital sexuality' — that is, the pattern and quality of the couple's sexual experience in their ongoing relationship and the meaning that sexuality has for them, both in general and in the vicissitudes of their sexual experience as a couple (McCarthy, 2002).

Sexuality in the couple relationship

To be human is to be sexual. An important element of the internalized sense of self that each person has will be a sense of themselves as a sexual person. This internalized sense of a sexual self will shape the meaning given to sexual experience, and the way the person expresses their sexuality.

The origins of a person's sense of sexual self are, not surprisingly, found in early childhood and in the culture of the family of origin. Kahn (1989) illustrates the childhood origins of our yearning for 'a sensual experience which reinvokes the sexual satisfaction previously experienced in infancy' with an evocative word picture:

It was dusk. The apartment was empty except for the two of them. As they lay entwined in a warm embrace, this room, this bed, was the universe. Aside from the faint sounds of their tranquil breathing, they were silent. She stroked the nape of his neck. He nuzzled her erect nipple, first gently with his nose, then licked it, tasted, smelled and absorbed her body odour: It was a hot and humid August day, and they had been perspiring. Slowly he caressed her one breast as he softly rolled his face over the contours of the other. He pressed his body close against her, sighed, and, fully spent, closed his eyes and soon fell into a deep, satisfying sleep. Ever so slowly she slipped herself out from under him, lest she disturb him, cradled him in her arms, and moved him to his crib. Having completed his 6 o'clock feeding, the 4-month-old had also experienced one more minute contribution to his further sexual development.

(p. 54)

This, suggests Kahn, underlines the point made by Freud's observation that 'No one who has seen a baby sinking back satiated from the breast and falling asleep with flushed cheeks and a blissful smile can escape the reflection that this picture persists as a prototype of the expression of sexual satisfaction in later life' (Freud, 1905).

Later, the capacity of the family to feel comfortable with sexuality, to talk about sexual issues in an age-appropriate way, and to respect appropriate boundaries around sexuality contributes to the emergence of an adult who is able to own and enjoy their sexual experience. Sometimes, sadly, childhood or adolescent experience includes sexual experience that is overwhelming or traumatic, and this has a lasting impact on the sexual self-image of the developing individual:

> As a boy, Bob was abused over a period of several years by an adult he looked up to and trusted. Coming from a family where he was already an emotional caretaker of his parents, he had no way of talking about his experience of abuse. The assumptions he made about himself as a result of the abuse — logical assumptions for his age and circumstances — remained the guiding principle through which he approached all sexual relationships as an adult. To be vulnerable in a sexual relationship was dangerous, but to be in control made it safe; to let his emotions be seen would lead to feeling shamed. Thus, for Bob, an impersonal, even aggressive, 'style' of sexual behaviour was safer.

In societies where romantic love is the accepted basis of forming a couple relationship, a search for a sense of wholeness seems to be a central part of the search for a partner (Mattinson, 1988). Individuals might express this as 'my other half' or 'my better half', and it is expressed somewhat more poetically by John Fowles:

> What I need from you is something inside you, between us, that makes half-living, half-loving . . . impossible.

(Fowles, 1977)

Kernberg (1995) suggests that sexual passion is the means by which the 'two parts' are temporarily fused, but without a loss of identity.

This requires the capacity to merge with the other, while still maintaining a separate identity. Herein lies a paradox:

> There is an intrinsic contradiction in the combination of these two crucial features of sexual love: the firm boundaries of the self and the constant awareness of the indissoluble separateness of individuals, on the one hand, and the sense of transcendence, of becoming one with the loved person, on the other. The separateness results in loneliness and longing and fear for the frailty of all relations; transcendence in the couple's union brings about the sense of oneness with the world, of permanence and new creation. Loneliness, one might say, is a prerequisite for transcendence.
> (Kernberg, 1995, pp. 43—44)

Kahn (2002), writing about the resolution of the Oedipal complex and described by Freud, refers to the capacity for experiencing 'tender and passionate feelings toward the same person' so that 'he or she could love who he or she desires and desire the one whom he or she loves' (p. 76). Maggie and Stuart demonstrated a split in their experience of love and sexuality in a particularly poignant way:

> They met and fell in love, and because of practical constraints started to live together quite quickly. Before they began to live together, Stuart told Maggie that he was bisexual; she decided that if they loved each other that need not be a problem. For some years it wasn't; but then there was a gradual increase of tension and arguments in their relationship. When they came for couple therapy, it became apparent that their differences in sexual orientation were proving difficult for both of them. Stuart had begun to have more frequent relationships with male partners and to experiment with longer relationships, rather than restricting himself to brief and largely anonymous encounters. Maggie had engaged in two affairs, passionate sexual relationships in which she felt 'desired as a woman'. When the therapist suggested that she found it difficult to experience affection and desire in the one relationship, this resonated strongly with her experience. Now they faced a situation in which there seemed to be no win—win outcome available. Continuing as they were, with both finding sexual fulfilment primarily outside their relationship with each other, did not fit with their values, especially since they now had two young children. To remain together with a commitment to monogamy meant a loss of the possibility for a sexually fulfilling relationship. To

separate meant that, even though they could remain friends and parents of their children, they would lose a relationship in which they both felt there was a great deal of love and affection.

But, in the context of a continuing couple relationship, what constitutes a 'good' sexual relationship? Whereas a few generations ago sexuality was still a largely taboo subject, Western societies have swung to the opposite extreme, with information about sexuality becoming almost de rigour in the popular media. Unfortunately, the nature of much of this information is dictated by a concern for sensationalism rather than by a desire to convey accurate information. Popular magazines give the impression that it is the number of sexual acts, along with some indefinable measure of their intensity, that is important. This runs the risk of replacing the old tyranny of guilt and shame resulting from a lack of knowledge with a new tyranny of 'unrealistic expectations and performance demands' (McCarthy, 2002).

Scharff (1982) has provided a helpful way of viewing of the role of the sexual relationship for the couple. Placing the emphasis on how well the sexual relationship serves the function of maintaining a sense of well-being in the couple relationship, he adapts Winnicott's (1960) phrase 'good enough mothering' as an analogy for 'good enough sex'. Like 'good enough mothering', such sex does not need to be perfect or flawless:

> Similarly reasonable goals for sexuality are that it be a useful, and on the whole enjoyable part of a marriage or relationship that is capable of containing and facilitating the average amount of conflict and frustration, giving *at some times* exactly what is needed and wished for . . . In the context of the needs of the larger family, the couple's sexual life should be adequate to allow them to feel sufficiently loved by each other that they, as parents, can give to their children.
> (pp. 10—11; emphasis in original)

The actual pattern of sexual behaviour that will serve this function for particular couples will vary enormously. What matters is not frequency of intercourse or intensity of orgasm, but the subjective experience of each partner. Each needs to feel that their sexual relationship is, on the whole, and despite occasional disappointments or failures, an enjoyable and bonding aspect of their relationship, which at times helps them to feel deeply reconnected with each other. The challenge for the therapist is therefore not obtaining factual data about a couple's sexual behaviour, but the more sensitive task of making it safe for the partners to talk about their sexual experience with each other.

A number of writers have suggested that how a couple engage sexually — the dynamics of their sexual relationship — provides the clearest indication of the dynamics of their relationship as a whole. Thus, for example, Skynner's description of his approach to family and marital therapy

> confronted with a presenting symptom, I expect to work back from the original problem, usually a complaint by or about one member to a more general emotional disturbance in the family as a whole, and then to the original pathology in the marital interaction and its expression in the sexual relationship.
>
> (Skynner, 1976, p. 141)

More recently, David Schnarch (1991) has described his approach to couple therapy as

> an elicitation approach to sexual and marital therapy. In an elicitation approach, couple's sexual behaviours (including style and content included and excluded in their repertoire) become a window into the whole of the partners' individual functioning and their relationship.
>
> Couples' sexual relationships contain a literal depiction of their lives, a metaphorical construction not unlike dreams. The analogy to dream interpretation is an apt one.
>
> (p. 146)

He continues, perhaps somewhat controversially:

> Just as the therapist never sees the actual dream content, it is neither necessary nor appropriate for the therapist to observe patients' sexual behaviour. It is necessary that the therapist obtain a graphically detailed report of the behaviour (or non-behaviour) and that he/she listen to the style and phrasing of the patients' report.
>
> (p. 147)

Whilst the 'graphically detailed' description Schnarch is advocating may not be necessary with most couples, it is important that the couple therapist is aware of the way in which relationship dynamics are enacted in the couple's sexual relationship.

Exploring sexual issues

Since it is an important part of the couple relationship, it is often helpful to put sexuality 'on the agenda' early in the therapy, if possible in the first interview, by making a general enquiry about the sexual aspect of the couple's relationship. People vary enormously in the degree of comfort with which they can talk about their sexual behaviour and experience, and couple therapists are no exception to this rule. Nonetheless, it is important that the couple therapist is able to talk in a relaxed and permission-giving manner with the couple about their sexual relationship. This will include being able to listen to the 'unspoken conversation' going on in the session — the emotional mood and the subjective experience that accompany the topic of sexuality. Skynner (1976) provides a simple and elegant example of the effectiveness of being able to talk, firmly but reassuringly, about the details of a couple's sexual experience:

> A late adolescent with schizoid traits, after some years of successful individual psychotherapy by a colleague to whom I referred him, married a lively and attractive girl. I was asked to see him again because of difficulty in the marriage, and a joint interview revealed that neither could take the initiative sexually and that both, because of their backgrounds, were too shy to speak about the problem to each other. A 'play-by-play' account of their interaction and sexual relationship revealed, among other things, that the wife's clitoral sensation was too intense and sensitive to permit direct pleasurable stimulation, though she could be excited by stroking of her pubis and other areas near the genitals.
>
> At the second joint interview they reported that they were enjoying sex more frequently and fully, and by the third session were able to discontinue treatment. The wife said that she had felt 'dreadfully embarrassed' at the first interview by my insistence on such detailed descriptions, but had begun to feel relaxed by the end of the first session and since then had been able to talk and act with her husband sexually with a freedom she had never thought she could attain.
>
> (pp. 135—136)

Essential ingredients for talking in such detail with couples about their sexual experience and behaviour will be the therapist's own level of differentiation of self with regard to talking about sex, and the recognition and careful maintenance of appropriate boundaries.

The therapist needs to be aware of, and able to contain and manage, his or her own erotic response to the sexual issues being discussed, and where necessary address those responses in supervision or in their own therapy.

Since sexuality is a private and sensitive topic for so many people, the therapist needs to avoid the collusion of using euphemisms. It is likely to be helpful if the therapist adopts the stance of an ethnographer, respectfully taking nothing for granted. For example, the therapist's assumptions about what is meant by terms such as 'foreplay', 'being intimate', and 'taking the initiative' — let alone more colloquial sexual language — can be different to the couple's; and there can be widely different meanings ascribed to such terms by different couples.

Finally, but by no means least, is the issue of the triangle that will be present in couple therapy unless a co-therapy pair are working together. In discussing sexual issues with a heterosexual couple, this triangle will always be unbalanced in terms of gender. This must be kept in constant awareness, and when necessary acknowledged in the therapeutic conversation. When talking with the partner of the opposite gender, the metaphor of the ethnographer and the stance of respectful curiosity are again helpful — and may often provide useful modelling for the same-gender partner.

As the dynamics of the couple's relationship begin to change, it is often helpful for the therapist to look for opportunities to explore how the changes being made are impacting on the sexual relationship. If, for example, a focus of the therapy has been on helping each partner to achieve a somewhat greater degree of differentiation of self — to be more 'their own person' and to have an appropriate sense of entitlement — the therapist can ask whether this is influencing their sexual relationship, and whether as a consequence they each are more able to own and enjoy their own erotic feelings in the presence of the other.

Responding to sexual difficulties

When a couple seek help with specific sexual difficulties during the course of couple therapy, the couple therapist needs to undertake an assessment to ascertain the nature of the difficulty, the extent to which it is a reflection of other difficulties in their relationship, and whether or not a referral to a therapist specializing in sexual difficulties is appropriate. An important consideration is whether the sexual dysfunction is primary (it has always been present for the partner concerned) or secondary (the difficulty has emerged now, but was not a part of sexual functioning either earlier in this relationship or in previous relationships for the partner).

> Michael presented with impotence, unable to maintain an erection during intercourse with his wife to whom he had been married for 13 years. Exploration of this problem revealed that he had actually never been able to have intercourse, including in relationships before he met his wife, but was able to maintain an erection during masturbation. He had consulted a medically qualified sex therapist, who had assured him that there was nothing wrong physiologically and had prescribed medication — but this had not worked.

Such a picture inevitably suggests the possibility of sexual trauma in childhood or adolescence, and this was indeed the case for Michael.

Annon (1974) describes four levels of intervention in response to sexual difficulties, giving rise to the acronym PLISSIT: permission giving, limited information, specific suggestions, and intensive therapy. In line with the discussion above, we consider it important that the couple therapist be able to provide intervention at the first two levels (permission giving and limited information), whilst the third and fourth levels (specific suggestions and intensive therapy) will depend upon the therapist's confidence in working with sexual difficulties and their level of training and experience.

Conclusion

An intimate relationship with a partner is intensely personal and touches on some of a person's deepest emotional yearnings and fears, as well as inevitably involving the sexuality of the two partners. Understanding the emotions involved, both in a relationship that is working well and in a relationship that is distressed, is important for the couple therapist. In this chapter we have provided an overview of some of the ways in which the experience of love can be understood, and have reviewed two recent ways of looking at the role of emotions in the couple relationship. We have concluded with some comments on the place of sexuality in the couple relationship, and some observations about responding to sexual issues within the context of couple therapy.

5

ASSESSMENT

Previous chapters have focused on a number of theories that seek to explain aspects of how couple relationships operate, and explored some of the ways in which those theories inform the practice of couple therapy. In this chapter and the three that follow the focus becomes more practical, beginning with the challenging processes of engaging the couple in therapy and forming an assessment.

Getting started: Engagement or assessment?

It is easy to take for granted and treat as routine processes that are commonplace for us, but which are often novel, bewildering, and involve anxiety for our clients. The couple therapist has to make decisions early in his or her contact with a couple who seek help (Hiebert, Gillespie, & Stahmann, 1993; Karpel, 1994). What type of difficulty seems to lie behind the initial problems they talk about? Is this a case that one can responsibly take on for therapy, given one's level of expertise and experience? Is it appropriate for one to see them in conjoint sessions, or should they see them separately — or refer one or both partners for individual therapy? Assessment is important, but the need for the therapist to assess and to make decisions must be balanced by an awareness of the anxieties and questions uppermost in the couple's mind. In addition, there is a need to engage with the partners in a way that makes couple therapy a process that elicits hopefulness that change is possible. This, of course, is not a dilemma unique to working with couples, but the strong affect and emotional volatility that often accompanies a distressed couple relationship sometimes makes this a particularly challenging task.

Often each partner is experiencing a number of different (and sometimes conflicting) hopes and fears: for example, hoping that going to see a therapist will be helpful, but fearing that it might be embarrassing or painful. They may be fearing that their relationship will be worse than ever when they get home after the session, and therefore wondering how they can balance honesty with caution in what they say to the therapist. What are they going to hear about themselves? Will they be asked to talk about things that are painful or confronting — about difficulties or disappointments in their sexual relationship or about the intimate details of the affair that they have had and now want to put behind them? How can they possibly begin to convey something of the complexity of 10, 20, or even 30 years of life together to a complete stranger in one brief session? When there has been so much hurt or disappointment, how can talking about things really make any difference? Whose side is the therapist going to take? Or perhaps there may be more aggressive wishes such as hoping their partner will be shown up, even shamed, or 'given a good talking to'. There is often the experience of, on the one hand, very much wanting to be listened to and understood; and, on the other hand, a perhaps slightly contradictory experience of wanting to be assured that the therapist knows what he or she is doing, that they are confident and competent, and that they will have some answers.

Virginia Satir, one of the great pioneers of family therapy, used to say in her family therapy workshops that she did not seek to make a *diagnosis* of a family that came to her for therapy. Instead, she would seek to gain an *appreciation* of the family in all its difference and uniqueness. She used the metaphor of a painting that caught her attention in an art gallery; her initial questions to herself as she looked at the painting would not be concerned with categorizing the painting or working out the school or tradition the artist belonged to — although those questions might become interesting later on — but rather she would be concerned with the unique impression the painting made on her, how it spoke to her, what emotions were touched within her as she looked at it.

We have a great deal of sympathy with Virginia Satir's metaphor of *appreciation* rather than *diagnosis* as constituting the essence of assessment. Obtaining information is important and necessary so that the therapist can make decisions about how to proceed with therapy. However, it is very easy to become so concerned with the content of the couple's difficulties, with categorizing their problem and seeking to know what to do, that the therapist can fail to develop an appreciation of the uniqueness of the experience that lies behind the story of the couple. A concern for appreciation, in the way that Virginia Satir was describing, leads to a focus on engaging with the couple, hearing their story, and wanting to understand their experience. This in turn will contribute to the formation of the 'therapeutic space' in which the partners can begin to feel safe enough to listen to each other, to explore their own and the other's experience, and then eventually to take risks with engaging differently with each other. We are advocating that the couple therapist try to develop and maintain a position that is akin to what self psychologists describe as an 'experience near' stance with the client (Livingston, 1995, 1999, 2001; Solomon, 1989; Wolf, 1988), seeking to become empathically attuned to each partner and to 'walk in their shoes' emotionally — although the need to be emotionally attuned to both partners simultaneously can make couple therapy particularly challenging! Thinking — analysing, categorizing, hypothesizing — will inevitably be going on in the background in the therapist's mind, and can also occur after the session; but the immediate priority when a couple enter our consulting room needs to be the process of engagement.

With that reminder about the importance of engagement with the couple at the beginning of therapy, this chapter will focus on the assessment process — the thinking and decision-making that needs to occur in the first phase of the therapy. The next two chapters will return to the question of how to engage the couple with a discussion of some of the skills involved in conjoint interviewing and of the therapeutic process in couple therapy.

The content of assessment: A five-dimensional framework

In earlier chapters a number of theoretical frameworks were reviewed that are of use to the couple therapist in seeking to understand a particular relationship. The question now arises: how is the therapist to know what information is needed, what questions to ask?

Our approach to this issue is to think of the couple relationship as a complex phenomenon whose reality cannot be captured by any one theory. Adopting a more holistic perspective, drawing upon a range of theoretical traditions, will therefore make it less likely that key issues will be overlooked. A framework is, however, needed for such a holistic approach so that relevant themes or issues suggested by different theoretical traditions are explored systematically rather than haphazardly. After gaining a broad picture of the relationship, it then becomes possible to focus in more detail on those aspects that seem to be important for understanding this particular relationship at this particular point in time.

A metaphor we use is that the relationship is like an irregularly shaped room that has a number of windows; looking in through each window reveals a different aspect of the complex whole of the room and of its contents. Each window can be seen as drawing upon a particular theoretical tradition to illustrate an important aspect of the functioning of the relationship. We are looking at one relationship but from different perspectives: no one view is more 'correct' than another, although some may prove particularly helpful when seeking to understand a specific couple relationship. The five dimensions that need to be considered — the five 'windows' — are described below. Together they serve to provide the therapist with a framework within which whatever knowledge he or she has available can be drawn upon as a guide for asking questions that will illuminate the functioning of the relationship in question. The five dimensions provide a way of operationalizing some of the ways of thinking about relationships from psychodynamic and systemic perspectives described in earlier chapters.

The developmental dimension

Key questions associated with this dimension concern the stage of development the relationship has reached, and how that might illuminate the current functioning and difficulties in the relationship. This leads the therapist to think in terms of the stages of the family life cycle (Carter & McGoldrick, 2005) and the developing pattern of the emotional relationship between the partners (Bader & Pearson, 1988), both discussed in Chapter 3. From the perspective of assessment, the first- and second-order changes associated with each stage of the family life cycle — the practical changes associated with particular stages, and the underlying changes in the patterning of relationships — are particularly important, since relationship difficulties often reflect a failure to negotiate second-order changes.

When thinking about developmental stages or patterns in relationships, it is important to keep in mind that the models or frameworks available are approximations that any particular relationship is unlikely to match exactly. It is important therefore not to allow the model or framework to define the reality of the particular relationship. Nonetheless, such frameworks can be extremely useful for generating hypotheses about a particular couple's or family's experience that can be further explored.

The cross-generational dimension

In this dimension the key questions concern the legacy that each partner has brought into adult life and into this relationship from their own family of origin (McGoldrick, Gerson, & Shellenberger, 1999; Searight, 1997). What indications are there about patterns of attachment that were acquired in early life and which still predominate (Crawley & Grant, 2005; Erdman & Caffery, 2003; Johnson & Whiffen, 2003)? What pointers to possible internalized object relationships can be discerned in the account of the family of origin of each partner, and how are these apparent in the present relationship (Framo, 1992; Scharff & Scharff, 1991)?

The communication dimension

The term 'communication' can have many meanings, and there is a considerable literature on the aspects of communication in intimate relationships from social psychology research (Duck, 1988; Duck & Dindia, 2000; Noller, 1984). More recently, research studies of the therapy process drawing upon aspects of discourse analysis have highlighted some of the complexities of the construction of meaning both in relationships and in the process of psychotherapy, including in couple therapy (Ferrara, 1994; Gergen, 1994; Muntigl, 2004; Silverman, 1997, 2001).

At a practical level, there are three areas of exploration that the couple's counsellor will often find useful in the assessment process:

- Drawing on the adage 'you cannot not communicate', how does this couple cope with the essential task of communication (Sieburg, 1985)? What are the strengths of their communication, and what appear to be areas of difficulty?
- Are there topics, experiences, or aspects of their relationship that seem to be avoided, or to raise anxiety if focused on? Given the practice wisdom that 'what cannot be talked about in a relationship hurts the most', what might lie behind such difficulties?
- As the couple communicate, are there instances discernable where 'the message sent does not seem to be the message received'? Are such instances examples of a 'simple' misunderstanding; or do they point to the impact of the unconscious, the 'invisible marriage', such as aspects of transference between the partners or of projection, influencing how the partners perceive and therefore ascribe meaning to each other's behaviour and communication?

The organizational dimension

How has this relational system been organized as a system (Minuchin, 1974; Nichols & Schwartz, 2001)? What is the hierarchical structure of the system? What roles are played by each partner, and what rules or norms seem to operate in the relationship? What types of boundaries seem to exist, and are the boundaries clear and recognized, or are they diffuse and frequently transgressed? What triangles or coalitions pre-dominate (Guerin et al., 1996)?

The ecological dimension

What is the wider context of this relationship? What cultural, ethnic, or socio-economic factors seem to be important in understanding the way the partners in this particular relationship live their life together (Searight, 1997; Hardy & Laszloffy, 2002)? How are their cultural and social values impacting on their struggles? What networks and supports are available to the couple, and what demands are placed upon them by the wider social system in areas such as work, finances, religious beliefs, and so on (Hartman & Laird, 1983)?

Running through these five dimensions is the important theme of *gender* — what is the male and female perspective, her story and his story, in each of the five dimensions? How are socially constructed gender roles impacting on the partners' expectations of each other and their respective roles in relation to paid work, childcare, and domestic responsibilities (Rampage, 2002)? How do these expectations engender conflict? What did each partner learn about being a man or woman in their family of origin and how is that impacting the current struggle? What are the power dynamics in the relationship and is there a gendered aspect to this (Ball, Cowan, & Cowan, 1995; Rampage, 2002)?

The structure of the assessment phase

When someone contacts a therapist for assistance with a difficulty in their marriage or relationship, the first decision the therapist must make is whether or not to begin with a conjoint session. Our clear preference is for a conjoint session for our first meeting with the couple, unless the partner making the initial contact expresses a definite wish to begin with an individual session. If conjoint work is the approach of choice when working with relationship difficulties (an issue we will address in Chapter 7), it makes sense to work in this way from the start whenever possible.

With an initial conjoint session the therapist can focus on the relationship from the beginning. The therapist experiences directly, from the start of the therapy, the reality of the relationship between the two partners, and is able to begin the process of making it safe for the partners to be together in the therapist's presence, talking about their different perceptions and experiences.

Usually, when it is explained that the therapist's preferred approach is to begin with a joint session, this will be accepted; however, should the partner making the initial contact still express a wish to start with an individual session, this should be respected. There can be a range of reasons why an initial individual session might be requested. Sometimes there are issues of control or of violence (actual or anticipated) in the relationship that lie behind the request, or the partner making contact may doubt their ability to voice aloud their concerns about the relationship in their partner's presence for fear of causing hurt or embarrassment. It is therefore important that a request for an individual session as the first contact be taken seriously, even if for the therapist it is a less-than-optimum way of commencing couple therapy. In some instances, as we will discuss in Chapter 7, it may well be that conjoint couple therapy is not the appropriate form of therapy — for example, where control or violence is an issue in the relationship or where there is an undisclosed affair. In other instances, the fact that the partner expresses a strong wish to begin with an individual session despite the therapist explaining their preference for beginning with a conjoint session may well in itself be communicating something important about the individual partner, or about the dynamics of the relationship, or about both.

The 'long route' and the 'short route' to assessment

In the majority of instances the first session will be a conjoint session, in which case there are two ways in which the assessment can be structured. First — which we term the 'short route' to assessment — the assessment may be completed in the first conjoint session. Occasionally the assessment may extend into part or all of a second conjoint session: Hiebert, Gillespie, & Stahmann (1993) describe a 'structured initial interview' that takes between one and four sessions to complete, depending on the complexity of the couple's history. There are sometimes good reasons for using the short route, principally where the time available for therapy is limited or where there are financial constraints on the number of sessions; indeed this used to be the usual format for assessment in couple therapy (Karpel, 1994).

There is now, however, a greater recognition of the value of an individual session with each of the partners as part of the assessment process (Karpel, 1994; Scharff & Scharff, 1991). In this format — which we term the 'long route' to assessment — the assessment phase of the therapy consists of an initial conjoint session, followed by an individual session with each partner, and then a second conjoint session. It is during the second conjoint session that the assessment process concludes, with the negotiation of an agreement about the ongoing therapy and the form it will take. The advantages of the long route to assessment include the following:

- The therapy will begin with a focus on the relationship rather than on one partner's experience or perception of the relationship. The therapist can see and experience the relationship *in vivo*, and can begin to gain some initial idea of the nature of not only the inter-personal interaction between the two partners, but also the unconscious marital interaction in the relationship (Ruszezynski, 1993).
- In the individual session with each partner, a more in-depth exploration of the partner's experience is possible, with less likelihood that what is said will be censored for fear of provoking or upsetting the other partner. There will be less of the reactiveness that is inevitable for some couples when they are in each other's presence, making possible a more reflective discussion.
- The therapist will have a better opportunity to establish a sense of rapport with each partner in the individual sessions, making it easier to respond empathically to both partners in subsequent conjoint sessions (Solomon, 1989). The individual session can be especially helpful in forming a therapeutic alliance with a partner who is initially ambivalent about couple therapy.

There is, however, one concern raised by the long route to assessment, namely the danger that the therapist is left holding a secret. The issue of secrets has always been a source of concern in couple therapy, although it is perhaps of greater concern when first learning to work with couples. In recognition of the difficulty posed by secrets, we always start a session with an individual partner (during the assessment process, as well as later in the therapy if further individual sessions occur) with a preamble along the following lines:

Before we begin, can I just check with you about the ground rules that I operate with. When I talk with one partner, I regard what is said as confidential, and I will therefore not talk with . . . about what we discuss today. If something comes up that I think it is important for the two of you to talk about, I will let you know; but it will be up to you to raise it with . . . , either privately at home or in a future joint session — I won't take the initiative and raise it for you. Also, I will let you know if there is anything in what you tell me that I think will make it difficult for us to continue with couples work.

Occasionally — but in our experience very rarely— some information is shared in an individual session that makes it difficult or impossible to proceed with integrity with offering ongoing conjoint couple therapy. The most obvious example (which will be discussed in more detail in Chapter 8) is when an ongoing and secret affair with a third party is disclosed (Cornwell, 2007; Moultrup, 1990; Weeks, Gambescia, & Jenkins, 2003). This creates a significant dilemma for the couple therapist, and a way must be found to resolve it. Since proceeding with conjoint therapy whilst one partner is involved in an ongoing but secret affair that the therapist does not know about is unlikely to lead to a successful outcome, it is probably preferable to have the individual sessions with the partners, to learn about the affair, and to deal with the issue directly at the outset of therapy with the partner who is holding the secret, rather than to continue on in ignorance. The possibility of occasionally encountering this difficult and 'messy' situation is, in our view, insufficient reason for not meeting with the partners individually as part of the assessment process. *but don't explain how you don't continue*,

Whilst we think that there are clear advantages in the long route to assessment, there are certain features of the couple relationship that, if the therapist becomes aware of them in the first conjoint session, make the long route to assessment essential rather than just preferable. These situations are as follows:

- There is reference to physical violence in the relationship, or the therapist senses that one partner imposes significant control or intimidation in the relationship. The issue here is one of a duty of care to explore issues of safety, including whether it is safe or appropriate to proceed with conjoint therapy; by definition, this exploration cannot be adequately or responsibly undertaken in the presence of a partner who is experienced as controlling or intimidating. Our approach in this situation is to take the position that an individual session with each partner is routine (and not negotiable — 'that's the way I work'). We also try to arrange the subsequent individual sessions so that we meet with the partner who might be subject to control or intimidation before meeting with the other partner; if intimidation or violence is confirmed, it is then important to structure the individual session with the violent or intimidating partner in such a manner that the situation is not made worse for the first partner.

- One partner is so emotionally distressed, perhaps at the possibility of the relationship ending, that they cannot participate in a conjoint session. An individual session with the distressed partner is then necessary in order to provide enough holding and containment for them to be able to tell their story in a coherent manner, and to decide whether it is appropriate to continue with conjoint sessions. An individual session with the other partner is necessary to maintain balance in the process, as well as to hear their story.

- It is indicated that an affair is part of the presenting problem. It is important for the therapist to explore what the affair meant to the partner involved, to clarify whether it has really ended, and to assess the extent to which the partner is still grieving the ending of the affair: all of these questions are difficult to explore in the presence of the aggrieved partner, who is likely to be both hurt and angry. It is often also necessary, as will be discussed in Chapter 8, to start the process of helping the aggrieved partner to begin to move beyond the stage of just reacting to the affair by exploring with them in a more reflective way their wishes for the future of the relationship. Again, this will be much more easily achieved in an individual session.

The process of assessment

There is, potentially, an enormous amount that the therapist can find out about a couple and their relationship that could be of use in understanding the couple's difficulties and providing help. The challenge is to find a balance between seeking information and engaging the couple in the therapy process in a way that begins the process of creating a 'safe space' for them. Each couple therapist will develop their own way of doing this. What follows is our approach, offered as a guide rather than as a prescription. The process we describe is one which is, deliberately, a relatively structured one. This structure helps to contain anxiety, and also facilitates the therapist in establishing control. For some couples it will also begin the process of helping each of the partners to think about their relationship *as a couple*, rather than being totally caught up in their own, often rather overwhelming, emotional experience — that is, it helps them to begin to achieve a 'couple state of mind'. This will be discussed in more detail in Chapter 7.

A guiding metaphor is to think of the assessment process as being about a number of stories that need to be told and need to be heard. We will comment briefly on each of the stories, in the sequence in which we usually invite them to be told. First, though, we need to emphasize that 'hearing the story' is not just a passive process of receiving information. The story will stimulate questions, which serve both to clarify and enrich the picture the story gives, and also to throw light on aspects of the marital interaction between the partners. The account given by Hiebert et al. (1993) of their structured initial interview provides a useful example of the range of questions that can be asked to help 'unpack' the stories told. The same authors also describe a style of 'dyadic questioning' — 'a process whereby the therapist asks one partner questions about the other' (p. 41). Whilst we do not routinely use dyadic questioning, it can be helpful with some couples in enabling each partner to think about their relationship rather than staying intensely focused on their own individual experience.

The story of the difficulties in the relationship

therapist est as hotel control
see P105
(1)

We start the first conjoint session by inviting each partner to tell us their account, one at a time, of why they are seeking therapy; for the couple, this is the obvious place to start. 'Warming up' with too much focus on other issues or asking other questions, in our experience, runs the risk of being experienced as a distraction or delaying tactic by the couple, and may to lead to impatience or increased anxiety. We usually leave it to the couple as to which of them tells about their experience of the difficulties first: the brief 'dance' over 'who goes first' that sometimes occurs can in itself be interesting, and may be worth exploring further at a later stage.

Hearing these two accounts of the story may take only a short while, or it may involve a long and complex narrative from one or both partners; the two experiences of the story may be very similar, or very different. Regardless, the story needs to be told: therapy cannot proceed until each partner has had an opportunity to tell of their experience as fully as they wish.

Jane responded to the therapist's invitation for one of them to tell him what had led them to make an appointment. She began to tell a long and complicated story, but did so in a way that was slow, never seeming to reach the end of any particular point in the story, and which left the therapist feeling that there was no natural point for him to move the focus to Bob's experience of their relationship. Beneath Jane's rather agonizingly drawn-out process of telling her story, he sensed considerable anxiety. He monitored Bob's non-verbal responses to what was happening, but Bob seemed intent on listening to Jane. About 5 minutes before the end of the session, the therapist finally — and in some desperation! — interrupted Jane, turned to Bob, and said something like 'Bob, you've been very patiently listening to Jane as she has told a rather complicated story. I'm keen to hear at least a little from you today about how you see things.' Bob's response was along the lines of 'I'm fine, and I'm so glad that you have listened to Jane. We went to see another counsellor who didn't listen, and she wouldn't go back to see him.'

We attempt to listen from a stance of respectful, concerned curiosity, asking clarifying questions as we feel we need to. We use this process, if necessary, to begin establishing the rule that each partner should be heard without undue interruption or correction by the other.

As with all stories, it is important to listen to the content, but it is equally important to listen to *how* the story is told. Does one partner seem to constantly defer to the other for permission to tell the story? What seems to be the underlying affect as the story is told — both for the one telling the story and for the partner who is listening (Johnson, 2004)? What countertransferential response to the story can we discern in ourselves — what sort of couple experience is being evoked in us as we listen (Scharff & Scharff, 1991), and what feelings are generated in us — sadness at the loneliness, envy at the passion and romance that once held so much promise, anger at the self-centredness displayed, or which of the many other possibilities?

The story of their relationship

Having listened to the story of each partner about their difficulties, we now need to place their relationship and its difficulties into context. We do this by asking a series of questions, the responses to which provide us with factual and demographic information, but which also provide further opportunities for reflective exploration. The questions we ask include the following:

- How old is each of the partners?
- What are their occupations?
- How long have they been together?
- Do they have children; and if so, how old are the children?
- Are they married or living in a de facto relationship? Did they live together before they married; and if so, for how long? How long did they know each other before they got married or started living together? How old were they at that time?
- Is this a first marriage or committed de facto relationship for each of them? If not, what are the details of their earlier relationships?
- When did each of them first start to have some private, inner concerns about how their relationship was working out?

This list is not exhaustive: each question has the potential to spark off another thought, another question, all with the common aim of getting to know *this* relationship, its vicissitudes, its strengths and successes, its unique history and circumstances. Have there been experiences of trauma, loss, or serious illness that have impacted on the couple's relationship (Johnson, 2002)? Again, whilst the content of the responses is important, it is the nuances, the hesitations, the meaningful glances, and the affective tone that are often more revealing through the clues they give to the marital interaction occurring at an unconscious level (Ruszczynski, 1993; Shaddock, 1998, 2000), and which will thus trigger off further lines of thought to be explored.

The story of how the partners engage with each other

How do the partners manage their everyday interaction with each other, especially in areas of interaction that can often be difficult for couples? We ask about three areas of interaction that both psychodynamic and systemic perspectives on relationships indicate couples need to negotiate: conflict and its resolution (Wile, 1993); vulnerability, being able to nurture and be nurtured (Johnson, 2004); and sexuality (Daines & Perrett, 2000; Schnarch, 1991).

With regard to conflict and vulnerability, we ask questions such as the following:

- How does each partner express their own anger and their vulnerability, and how do they experience their partner responding?
- How does each become aware of when the other is feeling angry or vulnerable, how do they respond, and how is that response received?

- How is conflict resolved — do things drift back to normal with nothing being said, or are the issues behind the conflict talked about?
- Who takes the initiative in resolving conflict and initiating reconciliation?
- Is there a sense of conflicts not being resolved, with information being kept and used again as ammunition in future arguments?

The issue of sexuality is raised at this early stage of the therapy for two reasons. First, in terms of process, couples vary enormously in the degree of ease or discomfort with which they can talk about their sexual relationship: in case the couple find this topic difficult or threatening, we want to include this issue in the discussion at an early stage, rather than leaving it hanging with the couple perhaps anxiously wondering whether it will be raised in later sessions. Second, in terms of assessment, there is a body of theory (Daines & Perrett, 2000; Scharff, 1982; Schnarch, 1991; Skynner, 1976), referred to in earlier chapters, that sees the couple's sexual relationship as containing and reflecting the core dynamics of their relationship. Thus, as the following example illustrates, information about the ways in which the couple interact around their sexuality can be important:

> The presenting difficulty was the way in which Francine felt smothered by Chris, who was reluctant to have Francine spend time alone with her girlfriends. Often at social functions Chris would become very tense if Francine seemed to be enjoying talking with people without involving him — especially if one of them was a male. Francine was the strong one in the relationship — successful in her career, very competent as a wife and mother of their two young children in the home environment. Underlying this strength was a marked need to be in control, and a well-developed pattern of taking responsibility for the emotional well-being of others, with a corresponding difficulty in asking for help or being seen as in any way vulnerable.
>
> Asked about their sexual relationship, an immediate air of tension and awkwardness entered the session. It gradually emerged that Chris had for several years struggled with premature ejaculation. Francine had 'done everything she could' to help him — which principally involved trying not to become sexually aroused herself in a bid to delay his orgasm — but felt defeated by the continuation of the problem. Chris had sought help on a number of occasions, with medical or behavioural solutions being offered

that did not lead to any improvement. Francine now had given up on the sexual dimension of their relationship — it was 'not important in the overall scheme of things'. Yet despite this avowed position, it quickly became apparent that this was both a very important and a very sensitive issue for her. She missed love-making, and she felt a failure for not being able to help Chris. This issue opened up a quite different view of the dynamics of their relationship, where it was Francine who began to emerge as the vulnerable and insecure partner, hiding enormous self-doubt behind her competent persona.

Dependent on the circumstances of the presenting complaint of the couple, we ask questions such as the following:

- How have they experienced the sexual dimension of their relationship, both in the context of their current difficulties and earlier in their relationship?
- How, if at all, have their present difficulties impacted on their sexual relationship?
- Are there specific sexual difficulties in the relationship (such as premature ejaculation or difficulty in experiencing orgasm), or a more general difficulty with desire or with being able to initiate sexual intimacy?
- Is there a pattern over who has taken the initiative sexually in the relationship, and has that changed over time?

The family-of-origin story of each partner

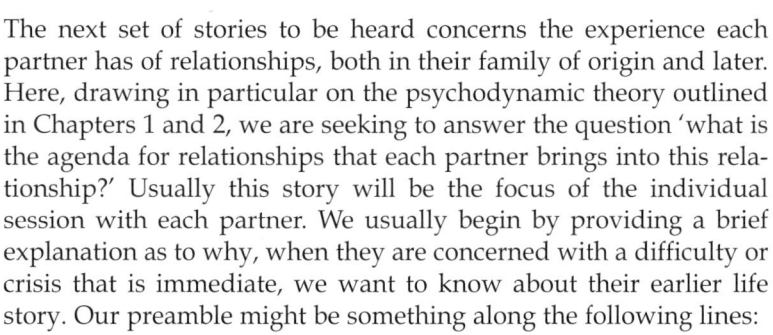

The next set of stories to be heard concerns the experience each partner has of relationships, both in their family of origin and later. Here, drawing in particular on the psychodynamic theory outlined in Chapters 1 and 2, we are seeking to answer the question 'what is the agenda for relationships that each partner brings into this relationship?' Usually this story will be the focus of the individual session with each partner. We usually begin by providing a brief explanation as to why, when they are concerned with a difficulty or crisis that is immediate, we want to know about their earlier life story. Our preamble might be something along the following lines:

It may seem a long way from your present concerns, but it would help me to know something about your family background —

that's because it is in our families, as children and adolescents, that we learn some important lessons about relationships; and what we learn can impact both on what we expect and on the way we respond in our later relationships as adults.

It is usually then helpful for the therapist to draw a simple genogram (McGoldrick, Gerson, & Shellenberger, 1999) as a way of organizing the information as the story is told. Once again, whilst the details are important, it is the way the story is told that is often most important:

- What are the nuances about the quality of relationships experienced in the family of origin, and how have they influenced the internalized 'agenda for relationship' of the partner?
- What can, and what cannot, be remembered; what hints might this give about the quality of early relationships?
- What are the idealizations, and what are the unresolved disappointments or hurts, that the person might seem to still be carrying?

We seek to make this a reflective discussion, where appropriate 'wondering aloud' about links between family-of-origin experience and the dynamics of their current relationship. The way in which such 'wondering aloud' about links between past and present is received can give valuable clues as to how open each partner might be to examining their own contribution to the difficulties in the relationship.

Since asking about family-of-origin experience involves a significant change of focus, a number of well-accepted models of couple therapy tend to view it as something that can be left until later, or even largely ignored (Jacobson & Christensen 1996; Johnson, 1996, 2004). Tempting though this might be, especially faced with a couple anxious to 'get on and change things', it can be a trap with serious consequences. We all too often come across clients who have seen other therapists who have never asked about — and therefore have not been told about — earlier life experiences of the client that are likely to be of critical importance in understanding their present dilemmas and symptoms. The most obvious example is that of childhood sexual abuse and its later impact on adult relationships. Other examples are earlier difficulties with mental health or serious physical illness, an experience of traumatic loss in childhood, or significant difficulties in a relationship with a parent.

David and Leanne were a couple in their mid-forties, both in senior and in demanding professional roles. They had been married for some 17 years, and had no children. They were concerned about a repeated cycle of arguments that seemed to be becoming more prolonged and emotionally draining as time went by. Part of the shared mythology of their relationship was that David had grown up in a family where relationships were difficult, whilst Leanne came from a more 'functional' and intact family; consequently, David was the one who had difficulty with communication in their relationship, and needed to change.

However, when exploring Leanne's family-of-origin story, it became apparent that there had been a number of prolonged painful experiences for her in early adolescence that she had kept to herself and struggled with — these experiences involved being bullied at school for being bright, coming from a different cultural background, and speaking with a strange accent; she was left feeling alone, different, and friendless. Her attempts to explain how unhappy she was to her parents had been met with advice that she heard as criticism, and with a lack of empathic understanding. She stated that she had never really talked to David about this time of her life, and didn't think that she could share with him now how painful this had all been for her — if she did, she would break down and cry, and he would see that as weak and contemptible. Yet after a couple of conjoint sessions, she took the risk of sharing her experience with David, and this led to a productive focus on how difficult it was for either of them to let themselves be vulnerable with the other for fear of ridicule (Leanne) or rejection (David).

We therefore regard the obtaining of a 'thumb-nail sketch' of the family of origin story of each partner as being an essential component of the assessment process in couple therapy (Crawley & Grant, 2005).

What is each partner wanting for the future of the relationship?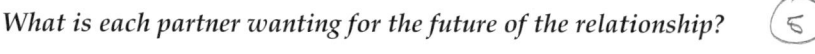

In the second conjoint session, the assessment process needs to be brought to a conclusion, with the therapist giving some feedback about the sense he or she has made of the stories that have been told, and with a dialogue about 'where do we go from here?' Should therapy continue beyond the assessment phase, and if so what form will it take? This is a point at which the commitment of the two partners to the relationship, both individually and as a couple, needs to be clarified; but this is more easily addressed now, after the reflective discussion that has already taken place in the preceding conjoint and individual sessions. The couple will often have some questions of their own at this stage. Typical questions concern how long therapy will take, whether future sessions are single or conjoint, and what steps can they take immediately to keep a fragile relationship intact. These questions need to be addressed as honestly as possible — which may well include the therapist saying that they do not know!

Conclusion

This chapter has outlined some of the ways in which the first meeting of the couple with the couple therapist is a novel and difficult situation for the couple. It has described how the primary task of the couple therapist is to engage with the couple in a way that begins the process of creating a 'safe space' in which the partners can talk more openly in the presence of each other than they are usually able to. An assessment process which explores five major dimensions of couple functioning was introduced that can guide the therapist in making a systematic assessment of the couple. We concluded by discussing the way in which we structure the assessment phase of couple therapy. Underpinning all of this is a conviction that what is most important in the first phase of the work with a couple is for both partners to feel that the therapist is seeking to understand each of them and their experience in the relationship, and is doing so within a framework of wanting to know without taking sides. This leads us into issues of technique in conjoint sessions that will be addressed in the next chapter.

— really like the 5 stage ass^t process.
provided structure within which
weeks imp material explored
— both feelings & emotional
commitment

6

TECHNIQUE

In this chapter we address some of the practical 'nuts and bolts' of conjoint couple therapy. We start with the challenge of creating a strong therapeutic alliance between therapist and couple, and then move on to look at some of the specific skills involved in conducting a conjoint session.

The centrality of the therapeutic relationship: Creating 'an island of safety'

The essential first task of the couple therapist is to transform the therapy session into a 'safe place' for the couple. That is, a place — physically, emotionally, and intellectually — where each partner can begin to feel that it is safe to express aloud and to share, and then to begin to explore, their own subjective experience of the relationship. As the safe space begins to be created, the therapist can then both use what emerges in that space — for example, the hints as to the transferences and projections that operate in the invisible marriage (Shaddock, 2000) between the partners — and also start to model a different way of being together:

> tolerance, taking in, reflecting, and digesting. These absorptive activities give us space to think and to analyse our own responses and countertransference. We model for the family this process of creating space for review. . . . This is our contribution to creating mental and emotional space in which many things happen and can be spoken and felt, but especially in which projections can be re-examined.
>
> (Scharff, D., 1989, p. 429)

For change to occur, this way of being together as a couple needs to happen first in the therapy sessions, and then to extend gradually to the couple's life outside therapy. In using the metaphor of the 'safe space' and describing the first task of couple therapy as the creation of 'an island of safety', we are drawing upon ideas from psychodynamic theory, and in particular the attachment theory concept of the 'secure base' (Bowlby, 1988; McCluskey, 2005; Sable, 2000) and Winnicott's (1965) idea of the holding environment. These ideas will be discussed further in the next chapter when we look at the therapeutic process in more detail.

Family systems theory suggests that the way a relationship is functioning at a point in time is a compromise that maximizes the benefits for each member, and minimizes the emotional cost or anxiety for each member (Hoffman, 1981; Minuchin, 1974; Nichols & Schwartz, 2001). Thus, even though the way a couple are behaving towards each other may seem illogical and counterproductive to the outsider, it has its own internal logic for the partners when viewed holistically and from within their own particular circumstances.

John and Mary, aged in their mid-thirties and with two young children, presented for therapy after Mary learnt of John's affair with a business colleague during a recent business trip. John, who was remorseful, was also aware that he had been unhappy with his relationship with Mary for some time: he felt that since the birth of their second child 4 years ago there had been little intimacy between them and they had been growing apart. He was ambivalent about whether he wanted the marriage to continue: perhaps they needed time apart to see if they really cared about each other and could regain a sense of intimacy. Mary was distraught, both by the discovery of the affair and by the prospect of separation. In the first two conjoint sessions, she lost no opportunity for attacking John, both for his deceit and disloyalty to her and for his questioning of the future of their relationship. It seemed as if anything John said led to a further outburst of sarcasm and rage from Mary. John would retreat further, assure Mary that he did love her, and repeat his suggestion of a period of separation.

What was the therapist to make of this situation? Was it hopeless? How could Mary possibly imagine that her attacking John so viciously would make him want to stay with her? What was the picture John had of intimacy that made him think that withdrawing and having a period of separation would lead to a renewal of intimacy between them?

The therapist, acting on the hypothesis that rage is a sign of an unbearable wound to the sense of self (Kohut, 1977; Livingston,

2001; Shaddock, 2000), persisted in wanting to understand something of what lay beneath Mary's rage. Gradually things started to
make more sense. For reasons that would later become clearer when
her family-of-origin story unfolded, Mary had always experienced
herself as an 'outsider', someone who was not particularly attrac-
tive or lovable to other people. Being John's wife was both a reassurance to her, and also a source of anxiety as at some level she was
waiting for the inevitable to happen and for John to turn away from
her. This, no doubt, explained in part why she had invested so
heavily in being a mother and had seemed increasingly unavailable
to John sexually and emotionally — the fear of his anticipated
rejection meant that the closeness she yearned for increased the
risk of rejection and hurt. Now it had happened: the sense of
wounding at a core level of her self was unbearable, and she
protected herself by reacting with rage — a desperate attempt to
shore up her self-esteem. As Mary began to talk a little more openly
than she had before about her fears and self-doubt, John's story also
began to make more sense. His commitment to Mary was actually
quite strong; but he grew up in a family where personal experience
or feelings could never be talked about, and he found the intimacy
and closeness he also yearned for both baffling and rather scary.
Sex, for him, was the only way in which he had ever really been able
to experience any sense of intimacy.

Part of the process of creating a safe space in couple therapy involves
enabling each partner to let go of their defensive position and begin
to look at their own contribution to whatever is happening in the
relationship that is proving disappointing or hurtful. When a couple
present for therapy for the first time, it is usually the case that each
partner believes that if only the other partner would change in some
way then things would be a great deal better. Mary certainly knew
that John was to blame, he had had an affair; getting to a point where
she could begin to explore the changes that *she* would need to make
in her sense of her own self-worth took time. John did not deny his
guilt over the affair, but beneath that he had an assumption that if
Mary was more available to him he probably would not have had the
affair; again it took time for him to start to own *his* difficulty with
being vulnerable and emotionally available in the marriage.
Generalizations should always be treated with great caution in therapy, but we have found it useful to always assume that *both partners
will need to make changes if the relationship is to change in a lasting way*:
we therefore look for opportunities of defining the process of therapy

in this way from the start. In this we draw upon Bowen's idea, discussed earlier in Chapter 3, that partners will usually choose a partner with a similar level of differentiation of self to their own (Kerr & Bowen, 1988; Titelman, 1998).

In talking of the importance of creating the 'safe space' in couple therapy, we are in part talking about what the literature describes as the therapeutic alliance. Research clearly indicates that one of the most important variables affecting the outcome of individual therapy, regardless of the model or approach used by the therapist, is the quality of the therapeutic alliance — the extent to which a conscious, collaborative relationship between client and therapist is established. This therapeutic alliance may be negotiated explicitly or implicitly between therapist and client (Bambling & King, 2001). It will involve three elements (Horvath & Symonds, 1991):

1. Establishing a bond, within which the client feels safe and understood, so that anxiety can be managed, and so that attachment to and trust in the therapist can develop.
2. Reaching a mutually agreed-upon understanding of what will happen in the therapy, expressing this in a way that makes sense to the client as a way of going about tackling their problem.
3. Negotiating an agreement about the goals of therapy.

When a strong therapeutic alliance is established, the client is more likely to feel held and contained, heard and understood (Bordin, 1979; Hubble, Duncan, & Miller, 1999; Wampold, 2001).

In the more complex situation of conjoint couple therapy, what form does the therapeutic alliance take, and does it play the same role? Research evidence about the crucial role of the therapist/patient relationship in individual therapy (Bambling, 2007) is not yet available to the same extent for couple therapy, but the issue is starting to receive more attention from researchers (Knobloch-Fedders, Pinsof, & Mann, 2004; Symonds & Horvath, 2004). Garfield (2004), drawing on this research, suggests that an important part of the therapeutic alliance in couple therapy is the emphasis the therapist gives to understanding and working to strengthen the allegiance of the partners to each other, the 'loyalty dimension' of their relationship, along with the relationship of each partner with the therapist. Thus, in couple therapy the therapeutic alliance involves not only the quality of the relationship of each partner with the therapist, but also the extent to which a sense of safety can develop for each partner in being present together in the therapy, as a couple.

Conducting the conjoint session

As indicated in the previous chapter, our preference is to begin our work with a couple with a conjoint session. For the therapist whose training has been in working with individual clients, this raises some immediate questions about how a conjoint session should be conducted. Whilst many of the principles of engaging with individual clients still apply, there are additional qualities or skills that the therapist needs when conducting a conjoint session. For the sake of clarity, we will look at these under four headings: control, empathic neutrality, adopting an interactive focus, and a capacity for 'negative capability' and curiosity.

Control

'Control' is not a fashionable word in therapeutic circles, but for the therapist conducting a conjoint session control is an important and unavoidable issue. Hiebert, Gillespie, & Stahmann (1993) describe it as being 'a critical issue' for all therapists and clients as to who is in charge of the therapy, and they go on to assert that 'The therapist must establish control rather quickly during the first session' (p. 5). First, though, we do need to begin by clarifying what we mean by 'control'. The usual association to the word 'control' is often one of authority, where one person tells others what they can or cannot do. When it comes to the process of conducting a conjoint session in couple therapy, that is only part of the story. Control — the therapist's control — is the outcome of the process of creating a new system, the temporary therapeutic system. In this new therapeutic system there is a different hierarchy — the therapist 'conducts' the session — and because it is a new system, it will have its own mores and rules governing interaction between the members of the system.

The new therapeutic system is, however, formed by modifying the existing system of the couple by the addition of the new member, the therapist. An existing system will at first attempt to restore a sense of homeostasis or balance in order to contain the threat posed by a change in its membership (Nichols & Schwartz, 2001). The therapist who joins with the existing system of the couple's relationship will be experienced as a threat, and the system of the couple's existing relationship will respond in ways that seek to neutralize the therapist's impact so that it can be 'business as usual' — despite the espoused (and, at one level, genuine) desire of the two partners to bring about a change in their relationship (Hoffman, 1981; Minuchin,

1974; Nichols & Schwartz, 2001). This process by which the existing couple relationship system seeks to contain the threat of the therapist will operate at a number of levels; it will sometimes be overt and obvious, and at other times exquisitely subtle. The rules and patterns of the existing system may, unless challenged, influence aspects of how the first session unfolds: who tells their version of the story first, how the story is told, what is included or not included in the story, what feelings can or cannot be expressed, what criticisms of one partner by another are allowed, and what meaning is attributed to events or experiences in the relationship. A primary task of the couple therapist — primary both in a temporal sense and in terms of importance — is to seek to be aware of when and how they are being recruited into the existing relationship system, and to facilitate instead the formation of a new, temporary therapeutic system. In this new therapeutic system, where the therapist rather than one of the partners in the relationship has the superior position in the system's hierarchy, different rules will need to operate, leading to the creation of the therapeutic system as a 'safe space' for both partners. Until this new therapeutic system is formed, there will be little prospect of the partners moving out of the established but unsatisfying, yet also well-known and safe, positions they typically take up in the relationship, or of new or different interactions occurring between them.

It is one of the paradoxes of conjoint couple therapy that once the therapeutic system is established with the therapist in control, it becomes possible for the therapist to 'give away' control and to be relatively non-directive. The therapist will then need to work to maintain boundaries in the new therapeutic system, and to provide holding and containment as the couple begin to take the risks that will be involved in engaging with each other in a more open and honest way. It is as if, once the therapist has established his or her control in the new therapeutic system, all can be confident that if things get too difficult, too scary, or too stuck, the therapist will be able to intervene effectively to restore the process. Without control having been established by the therapist in the early stages of the therapy, this confidence will not exist.

The ways in which a therapist establishes control in the early stages of the therapy will depend on a number of factors, including the personality of the therapist and his or her experience and confidence in their professional role in the conjoint session. The characteristics of the two partners in the relationship and their level of anxiety will also be critical; the greater the anxiety, the more likely it is that there will be an attempt by one or both partners to reduce anxiety by dominating or controlling the session. For example, one partner may attempt to talk at great length, leaving the other partner no opening to participate in the discussion unless the therapist takes control and 'directs the traffic' in the session. Or one partner may declare angrily, or in a powerless but passive-aggressive manner, that they see little point to the session and have only come because their partner insisted. This invites the therapist into the trap of either getting into a power struggle with that partner, or allowing the session to become organized around trying to persuade that partner to participate.

Often the therapist will be able to establish the hierarchy and rules of the new therapeutic system in an unobtrusive manner that, when done skilfully, will scarcely be noticed. For example, an introduction along the following lines establishes the therapist as setting the initial agenda:

See Pg 1 & Ass⊤ Shapee

I guess what needs to happen in this first meeting is for me to hear what has been happening for the two of you that has resulted in you two coming to see me today. I imagine that you will each have your own view on that, and it's important that I hear both points of view. Which of you would like to start?

Sometimes there will be a move by one partner to control the agenda of the session or to reassert the rules of the couple's relationship system in some way, and this can give the therapist an opportunity to reinforce gently the hierarchy of the new therapeutic system. For example,

Mary: Why don't you tell (the therapist) about what you did when we first moved in together . . .

Therapist: Yes, I think it may be important to talk about that, but before we do, I would like to hear what else John has to say about . . . (whatever John was saying before Mary interjected); *or*: Well, it sounds as if that is something that is important to you, Mary; would you tell me what you remember about whatever it was that happened then?

On some occasions the therapist will need to directly confront one or both partners about their contribution to the session, and occasionally this will need to be quite direct or even forceful. This is most likely to be the case where there is a great deal of anger in the session — anger that will almost inevitably be a cover or defence against some more vulnerable or distressing experience. A useful guide is 'the principle of least contest' — that is, the therapist using only just-enough assertiveness or 'force' to achieve his or her goal, knowing that they can always make another attempt, with greater assertiveness, if they need to. Thus, a mild

Challenge to one too angry

> John, could you just hang on a minute; I'm anxious to hear Mary's point of view as well as yours.   *1st challenge*

is preferable to an outright confrontation with John. It is, however, important that the therapist is able, *if necessary*, to confront John with sufficient strength and determination to ensure that Mary does get heard:

2nd more forceful challenge.

> Whoa! Stop! Hang on a moment. John, we have a problem. If I am going to be able to help the two of you, it's important that we can each talk without too much interruption. I know it is difficult for you at the moment, but I want you to sit back and *listen* to what Mary is telling me. If you disagree with her, I'll make sure you have an opportunity to talk about that afterwards. Is that alright?

For some therapists, this need to confront can present a challenge because of their own, perhaps unconscious, anxieties or prohibitions about being assertive or challenging to others, or because of their own agenda about being a rescuer or peace-keeper in the face of another person's anger or emotional distress.

Empathic neutrality

'Neutrality' is another word that has come to be viewed with some scepticism in psychotherapy in recent years; postmodernism alerts us to the complexities involved in the construction of meaning in any social encounter, let alone one as difficult as a conjoint therapy session, and to the impossibility of any ultimate neutrality in the way we construe situations. Nonetheless, as with the idea of control in the conjoint session, an awareness of the philosophical limitations of the idea of neutrality must be balanced by an awareness that neutrality will be an important issue for the couple, and its perceived presence or absence will strongly influence the way in which one or both partners will experience the session.

The idea of a therapist being neutral sometimes conveys a sense of being uninvolved, of unresponsiveness, even of coldness. We have

neutral & empathic

therefore added the adjective 'empathic' to the word 'neutrality' to try to convey the essence of the stance the couple therapist needs to take with the partners. In the conjoint session there are three subjective realities that the therapist must engage with — that of each of the two partners, and the relationship. In the early stages of the therapy in particular, the therapist will need to *actively* move backwards and forwards between the two partners, seeking to engage empathically with each whilst also recognizing that the other's experience will be different. At the same time, the therapist will need to be seeking to hold in mind the nature of the relationship and how that might be experienced by each. And all of this whilst not being experienced as taking one partner's side against the other!

> So, Jane, I'm hearing you say that you feel very torn about what you want for the future of your marriage — you realize that leaving Mike will be an enormous step for you, and very painful for him, but you feel quite trapped at the moment and can't see any real possibility of the way you feel about Mike changing. Have I understood you correctly? ... And Mike, I imagine that it is very hard for you to hear that from Jane? You probably see the situation very differently, you are incredibly anxious to try to find a way forward that enables you and Jane to stay together, you are very frightened of losing her — have I got that right? ... So I suppose that it must feel very tense and awkward, very tense and uncertain, for you both as a couple at the moment, with perhaps a sense that anything you say, any move you make, may be misunderstood, taken the wrong way — or even cause more hurt. Is that what it's like for each of you? Could you help me to understand that a bit more?

her views / his views / affect / a / both / ↓ / Jane more info

To understand something of the complexities of maintaining a neutral position whilst also being empathic, we need to review some ideas from systems theory introduced in Chapter 3. The new therapeutic system of 'couple plus therapist' that is formed at the beginning of couple therapy consists of three people, and presents abundant opportunities for the creation of triangles — which, like all triangles, will possess great potential for becoming dysfunctional (Kerr & Bowen, 1988; Guerin et al., 1996). The basis of some of these triangles are obvious — two women and one man or vice versa, one 'guilty' party and two others, one partner who wanted to see a therapist (and who may be implicitly assumed to be aligned with the therapist) and one who did not, and so on. Other triangles are idiosyncratic to the particular couple — for example, one partner may work as a therapist or in a related field and the other be an 'outsider', or there may be some perceived demographic basis for one partner to have an alliance with the therapist. Triangles can develop unexpectedly during the early stages of the therapy; for example, when one partner is more articulate about their emotional experience or about what they want from therapy. Any of these situations can easily create the potential for the therapist being seen to be aligned more with one partner than the other. Neutrality requires the couple therapist to act in a way that does not consciously favour one partner over the other (Cecchin, 1987), but the core of the issue of neutrality in couple therapy lies not in some imagined objective measure of the therapist's even-handed behaviour, but in the subjective experience of the partners. The therapist has succeeded in being neutral if each partner, asked after the session by a friend 'so whose side did the therapist take?', responds in a thoughtful manner 'I'm not really sure.'

To achieve this 'perceived neutrality' the therapist may well need to invest different, rather than equal, amounts of time and attention in each partner in the early stages of the therapy process. For example, the therapist may become aware that one partner is very resistant to the idea of therapy or to the idea that there is a problem with the relationship that they cannot fix themselves. The therapist may choose to spend more time talking with that partner in an attempt to understand his or her experience of the relationship and of the interactions that the other partner identifies as problematic. This will need to be done carefully and thoughtfully: the therapist will want to be cautious about not giving too much control to the reluctant partner, and to be careful not to alienate the 'available' partner. The therapist will, however, be wanting to get across the message that both partners have valid perspectives on their situation and that a way through the impasse needs to be found if there is to be progress for their relationship. As we have already suggested, to achieve this the therapist will often need to actively 'go backwards and forwards' between the partners, making empathic responses to confirm that they have understood one partner's experience, whilst also recognizing that the other's experience will be different. The need for *concurrent* empathic engagement with the often very different experiences of the two partners, *whilst also* being able in their own mind to stand outside the experience of the two partners and to 'hold in mind' — think about — the couple dimension of the relationship, is one of the most challenging aspects of the couple therapist's work.

Adopting an interactive focus

Another difficult skill to master for the therapist who is new to conjoint work with couples is that of maintaining an interactive focus in the session. This involves finding a middle position between doing individual therapy with one partner in the presence of the other and allowing the couple to interact. The difficulty in simply encouraging interaction is that the couple is likely to recreate their systemic pattern of interaction with little that is new or different emerging. The therapist needs to witness enough of the interaction to gain a working knowledge of the couple system, but then needs to intervene to assist something different to happen.

In working with groups, a common piece of practice wisdom is that the one place the skilled group leader will *not* be focusing is on the group member who is currently speaking. The group leader's task — whether in a committee meeting or a therapy group — is to facilitate the responses of other group members to what is currently being said, and to do this they need to be monitoring the non-verbal responses being communicated by other group members.

In conjoint couple therapy, the therapist is in much the same position as the group leader. When Mary is speaking, the therapist needs to use all their available skills to attend to, empathize with, and understand what she is communicating. *At the same time*, John's non-verbal response to what he is hearing from Mary provides vitally important information *about their relationship*. What affective clues are there in John's non-verbal behaviour? What is the therapist's own internal response, not only to what he or she is hearing from Mary, but also to John's non-verbal response? For example,

- Mary is talking in a rather complaining and critical way about her disappointment with the way she and John now seem emotionally very distant from each other.
- The therapist listens to the details of Mary's story, senses a degree of loneliness in her beneath the criticism, and asks Mary about this; she pauses, then says she had not really seen it that way before, but she supposes she is lonely, and she begins to quietly shed some tears; the therapist is aware of feeling more in touch with Mary as she does so — it is as if she has stopped hiding part of herself behind a familiar story about John's shortcomings.
- At the same time the therapist has been aware of John's air of impatience and boredom — 'here we go again' — as Mary is going though her list of complaints; he is aware of feeling rather

irritated at John's response; he then notices John's slight tensing as Mary acknowledges that she is perhaps lonely and begins to shed some tears. John makes a rather defensive comment about his demanding work schedule and how he is now trying to keep at least part of the weekends free from work.

- The therapist, curious about John's apparent tensing when Mary began to cry and aware of his irritation with John in the counter-transference, decides not to comment on the content of the discussion by asking about Mary's loneliness or about John's work (which could have led to his being invited to take one side or the other in their recurring conflict); instead he asks John, in a curious and interested way, 'John, what was it like for you just then, when Mary began to cry? What happened for you, what did you experience?'

- John's initial response is irritable and defensive — 'I can't see why she would be lonely, she's always doing things with her friends' — but the therapist tries to reach beneath that initial response to a see if something more vulnerable was touched on for John — a vulnerability that Mary probably would not see very often.

A useful rule of thumb in conjoint work with couples is for the therapist to engage for long enough — sometimes only a couple of sentences, or sometimes a more protracted dialogue — with one partner *until* there is something that is perhaps new or different for the other partner to respond to or react to; and then to explore that response or reaction. Thus, in the example above, the therapist suspects that Mary's admitting to loneliness (a vulnerable experience) and shedding some tears about it might be something that Mary does not often allow to happen — particularly in front of John. John's body language suggests that he is used to 'sitting out' complaints from Mary, conveying a rather passive-aggressive boredom as he does so, and then justifying his own position. The therapist's hunch is supported by his awareness of John tensing when Mary became upset and by John's rather defensive response to Mary. Exploring John's experience when Mary momentarily behaves in this different way by allowing her vulnerability to be glimpsed has the possibility of opening up a different discourse between them, from which something new might emerge.

A capacity for 'negative capability' and for curiosity

Bion (1970) used the term 'negative capability' to describe a way of being in a state of free-floating reverie, 'without memory or desire', so that the psychoanalyst can be in a state of mind where he is receptive to whatever comes into his mind in relation to the patient. He took this term from a letter written by the poet John Keats to describe Shakespeare's poetic creativity: '...Negative Capability, that is, when a man is capable of being in uncertainties, mysteries, doubts, without any irritable reaching after fact and reason' (cited in Symington & Symington, 1996, p. 169). The aim is for the therapist to

be as open as possible to what the patient brings to the therapy in the here-and-now of each moment. Clinging to theory prejudices the therapist to hear what the theory teaches should be heard. Feeling too tied to exactly what the patient said in the previous session prejudices the therapist to hear what has already been said and to learn what is already known. Only by abandoning what is already known as fully as possible can therapist and patient be open to what is not yet known.

(Scharff & Scharff, 1998)

Although both Bion and the Scharff & Scharff are talking about psychoanalysis or psychoanalytic psychotherapy with individuals, a capacity for 'negative capability' is also an important quality for a couple therapist to possess. Conjoint sessions are often filled with complicated emotionally charged interactions and competing agendas. These make it particularly important that the therapist be able, from time to time, to 'stop' and 'just be' in the session, to be open to whatever subjective experience the couple are generating within the therapist. Moments of feeling lost, confused, or not understanding why something is as important as it appears to be, all contain the seed of a new quality of understanding — if the therapist can resist the temptation to 'know' from theory, to impose order on disorder, to find a solution. At such moments therapy easily becomes rather like being lost in a strange city — we look anxiously and even frantically around for something we recognize that we can use to orientate ourselves, but in doing so we are unable to notice what is actually all around us.

It is useful for the therapist who is starting to conduct conjoint sessions with couples to assume that every session is *always* an exercise in cross-cultural exploration: *always*, because one of the easiest traps to fall into is that of assuming that we know. Two people, who have been in an intimate relationship with each other for a number of years, will have an enormous amount of shared experience to bring to a therapy session. The similarity of some aspects of that experience to the therapist's own experience and the subtle pressures to demonstrate expertise can easily tempt the couple therapist into taking short cuts, into assuming that he or she understands what the partners mean by the words and phrases they use. A more productive stance is that of being curious, indeed of taking the role of the 'naïve inquirer' (Buirski & Haglund, 2001):

- 'When you say that you want to be more intimate with John, what picture do you have in mind of what would happen differently between you and John?'
- 'Can you describe *how* you show Mary affection when you come home from work?'
- 'You are obviously very angry and you say that you've had enough of this relationship. In my experience, different people often mean different things when they say that. I wonder what it means to you?'

Carlos was a tough man, in a career that was a man's world; he had grown up with a father who was, literally, a Sergeant Major. There had been some angry exchanges between Carlos and his partner, culminating in Carlos pushing her into a wall; as a result Carlos had in the past attended group sessions about anger management for men before seeking couple therapy with his partner. In a couple therapy session he described how he was now trying to respond differently to his partner but often still found himself reacting angrily when she criticized him. He described a recent row that had erupted as soon as he walked in the door — he had asked his partner how her day had been and she had responded by telling him that their two young children had driven her to distraction: he had become angry. In talking about this incident, he was able to recognize and put into words that he initially felt guilty for not being there for his partner when he heard about her day, but this had almost instantaneously flipped over into anger.

The therapist was able to not assume that he knew what Carlos meant by 'feeling guilty', but instead spent some time exploring with him the subjective experience he labelled as 'feeling guilty'. This led to a recognition that it was actually shame that Carlos had experienced, not guilt, and that shame was a very familiar experience for him in his relationship with his demanding and often rather punitive father when he was young. The emotions of guilt and shame are often confused by people, but are in fact different. Recognizing the difference between shame and guilt opened up for both Carlos and his partner an exploration of a whole new dimension in the experience of their relationship.

One of the most useful metaphors for the role of the couple therapist is that of the therapist as an ethnographer. An ethnographer seeks to understand an unknown culture by immersing themselves in it and by making no assumptions about meaning (Hammersley & Atkinson, 1983). Every facet of the culture being studied — even though it might seem quite familiar and therefore obvious to the ethnographer — is questioned rather than taken for granted. The aim is to understand the culture *in its own terms*, using its own descriptions and explanations, rather than in terms of the ethnographer's own taken-for-granted knowledge.

The metaphor of the ethnographer provides a valuable guideline for conducting the conjoint session in couple therapy. Beginning couple therapists often get rather anxious after the initial stories have been told — 'what do we talk about now?' is the spoken or unspoken question they hear from the couple, and it is easy to slip into problem-solving or making suggestions at that point. In reality, there is always an enormous amount the therapist does not know about the couple and their relationship. As we will consider in the next chapter, even the most trivial of daily events in the couple's life can, if approached in a 'not knowing' and curious way, open up discussion that illuminates aspects of the dynamics of their relationship for fruitful further exploration.

Conclusion

In this chapter we have considered some of the skills involved in conducting the conjoint therapy session in a way that leads to a focus on the relationship. This requires attention to some particular issues: establishing control of the new therapeutic system, seeking to enable both partners to experience the therapist as neutral, and maintaining an interactive focus in the session. The couple therapist also needs to be able to take on the role of 'naïve inquirer', the ethnographer, instead of assuming that they know what the couple are referring to when they talk about their experience of their relationship. Developing and using these skills will make it more likely that the couple therapist will be able to make the conjoint session a safe space in which the two partners can take risks with self-disclosure and can explore together aspects of their relationship in a new way.

7

THERAPEUTIC PROCESS

In the previous two chapters we have described an approach to assessment in couple therapy, and also some of the skills involved in conducting conjoint sessions. In this chapter we address a number of issues to do with how the couple therapy session is structured, beginning with the question of whether there are discernible stages to the therapy process once the assessment is completed.

Stages of therapy

First-order and second-order change

At the root of thinking about progress and change in couple therapy is the distinction between two forms of change in the couple's relationship, between first-order change and second-order change (Watzlawick, Weakland, & Fisch, 1974). First-order change refers to a change in behaviour that is a response to the therapy situation, but which is not based on any underlying change in the pattern or dynamics of relationships between the partners or within the family. For example, after a few sessions a couple might report a decrease in the frequency of conflict between them. However, such change often does not last once the therapy ends.

Contrasted to this is second-order change, which occurs when there is a significant shift in the underlying patterning of relationships. This change in the relationship system results in the problem or the symptomatic behaviour becoming redundant. We argue that second-order change in relationships, whilst discernible in the pattern of interaction between the two partners, has as its basis a change in the way the parties to the relationship perceive and respond to each other. This is usually a consequence of a change in the sense of self of one or both partners. The new and less problematic pattern of interaction, in turn, leads to further growth and consolidation in the partners' sense of self. For example, it is usual in couple therapy that each partner will enter therapy believing, at some level, that if their partner would change in some way then their problems would be lessened or resolved. Initial attempts at change are likely to be based — consciously or otherwise — on bargaining or accommodating to the other: 'if I do x, you will have to do y'; however, such attempts at best usually only lead to first-order change. Second-order change is more likely to begin when each partner reaches a point of wanting to behave or respond differently in the relationship, because the new behaviour is more congruent with the person they want to be in the relationship. This usually involves them in taking more responsibility for their own experience and behaviour in some way, and focusing on this rather than on changing their partner.

Mark found Susan's angry criticism of him difficult to take, and his usual response was to make a half-hearted attempt to argue his case, but then to withdraw, which would inevitably inflame Susan's anger; she would pursue him and attempt to get an answer from him, and he would go further into his shell. Each blamed the other, and demanded that the other change. Mark insisted that if Susan stopped being so critical and unreasonable, then he would be able to talk with her and sort issues out, whilst Susan was adamant that if Mark would face up to issues she would not need to get so angry.

On one occasion, after some weeks of therapy, Mark reported that they had had a major fight the previous weekend. This caught the therapist's attention — Mark would usually describe Susan as having been upset or angry, not 'us' having a fight. Asked to elaborate, Mark described a situation where 'I don't know what happened, but I felt I had just about had enough. I told her she had no right to be so bitchy to me — we had quite a shouting match.' The fight had not lasted long — certainly not a fraction of the time usually spent in sullen silence after Mark had distanced from Susan. They felt they had sorted something out for once, and they had seemed to get on better afterwards as a result. Susan reported that she did not like fighting with Mark but the row that they had was certainly better than his usual pattern of behaviour.

This was the start of a new phase for them as a couple. Something had changed in Mark so that he no longer felt intimidated by Susan's angry criticism, but now felt able to assert his position, with anger if necessary. Mark was starting to re-engage in the relationship.

The creation of the safe space with a solid therapeutic alliance is, as we argued in Chapters 5 and 6, the vital foundation for change in the couple relationship. However, the de-escalation that accompanies this is only first-order change, where '... the way the interactions are organised remains the same, but the elements of the cycle are modified somewhat' (Johnson, 2004, p. 19).

De-escalation, re-engagement, and softening

A useful way of thinking about how the therapeutic process of couple therapy develops over time is provided by EFCT, which was introduced in Chapter 4. Johnson (2004) describes the change brought about by couple therapy conducted according to the EFCT model as involving three sequential 'shifts' in the couple's relationship:

- First, there is a process of *de-escalation of the negative cycle of interaction* in the relationship, as the therapist creates an alliance with the two partners and slowly and empathically 'unpacks' the negative interactional cycle that expresses the core conflict over attachment between them.
- Second, there is a process of *re-engagement in the relationship by the withdrawn partner*. This partner begins to be more assertive about their experience in the relationship, and about expressing their needs and wishes; they start to exercise more control in the relationship and to be more emotionally available.
- Third, there is a process of the 'blaming' partner *softening* — that is, the more hostile, critical or attacking partner taking the risk of owning and exposing their own vulnerability in a way that facilitates emotional bonding and a rebuilding of trust in the relationship.

Johnson (2004) points out that whilst these can be described as three separate and independent events, in the actual process of the therapy they

> are, of course, interwoven and reciprocally determining. As a critical spouse becomes less angry, the less engaged partner risks more involvement; as this involvement increases, the critical spouse allows him- or herself to disclose needs and desires more openly. This then makes it easier for the less engaged partner to be more responsive.
>
> (p. 19)

In our experience this description of the three 'shifts' in EFCT has an application beyond the EFCT model. There is a logic about the sequence, and it can often provide a useful 'mud-map' that helps orientate the couple therapist no matter which framework they are using. To take the risk of expressing vulnerability, especially for the partner who has hidden their vulnerability behind being angry and attacking, or critical and 'in the right', requires a degree of confidence that the other partner will be there for them. A re-engagement by the withdrawn partner, indicative of a stronger sense of self and of emotional entitlement in the relationship by that partner, therefore needs to come *before* the more dominant partner can lower their defences and take a more vulnerable position. Thus, even when working with couples in longer-term therapy, the framework of EFCT's 'three shifts' is a useful one to keep in mind.

Who do we talk to? Individual versus conjoint sessions

Implicit in what has been said in earlier chapters is an assumption that the norm in couple therapy is to involve both partners in conjoint sessions. At an intuitive level it makes good sense to have both partners present in order to resolve the difficulties between them. At the same time, the prospect of having two people who are in disagreement or emotionally intense conflict with each other present in the session is often a daunting prospect for the therapist — something that it makes equally intuitive good sense to avoid! The current practice of conjoint sessions for couple therapy has not always been the norm. Prior to the 1950s, much work with couples that involved more depth was conducted with each partner being seen separately for therapy, either by the same therapist or each by a different therapist (Nichols, 1988). Conjoint sessions then gradually became more common, both in psychoanalytic marital therapy and particularly in family systems approaches.

There are, however, situations where individual sessions with each partner are necessary because of the dynamics created by the difficulty in the couple's relationship. There is also the reality that for some couples, particularly where marked difficulties in personality are involved, it is not possible to create the safe space necessary for conjoint therapy. In such circumstances, referral for individual therapy for one or both partners may be necessary. Sometimes a referral for individual therapy makes conjoint couple therapy a viable proposition at a later date.

Some individuals, despite clearly needing help for personality difficulties or perhaps suffering markedly from depression, anxiety, or some other mental health condition, cannot bring themselves to seek individual therapy, but may allow themselves to become involved in couple therapy — often on the conscious assumption that it is their partner who is the real problem! Reaching a point where such a person is able to accept a referral for individual therapy may constitute the most successful outcome to their seeking help as a couple that can be achieved.

There may occasionally be circumstances (particularly, for example, in isolated areas of a country like Australia) where referral is not possible, but neither is conjoint therapy, and one therapist will work individually with both partners. Very careful consideration must be given to the issue of boundaries in this situation, and careful 'ground rules' for the therapy worked out. For example, it is usually important that it is understood that the focus of the sessions will be on the individual who presents and on their perception or experience of their partner; and that the partner *per se* will not be talked about, particularly in terms of attributing motivation or attitude.

Some approaches have developed that make deliberate use of individual work with partners to a relationship along with conjoint sessions. The best-known such approach is that developed at the Tavistock Institute over many years (Ruszczynski, 1993). In this approach a co-therapy pair work with the couple, one with each partner and initially in individual sessions. There are, however, occasional joint sessions involving both partners and both therapists, determined by the needs of the couple and the progress of the therapy. The essence of the work is the therapists' monitoring and use of the reflection process that develops, whereby the unconscious dynamics of the couple's relationship is experienced by the therapists in their own countertransference to each other. This process has clear similarities to the reflection process in supervision (Heimann, 1950; Searles, 1955), where in a parallel process unconscious aspects of the therapist/patient relationship will be recreated in the supervisor/supervisee relationship. A not dissimilar structure, involving two therapists and a careful blend of individual and conjoint sessions, has been developed by Jenkins (1990; 2007) in his work with couples with violent relationships, although he works in a narrative rather than a psychodynamic framework.

The situation can also arise where it appears it would be helpful for the couple therapist to have individual sessions with one or both of the partners during the course of conjoint couple therapy.

Although once frowned upon, this is now recognized as a necessary step in the process for some couples. We suggest that the following guidelines should be followed:

- The therapeutic alliance and therefore the focus of the therapy remains centred on the couple relationship, and individual sessions are only offered if there is a need to remove a 'road-block' to the conjoint therapy. Usually only a few sessions will be necessary, otherwise referral for individual therapy should be considered.
- Individual sessions should be offered to *both* partners if the relationship is volatile and/or there is a possibility that the other partner will, consciously or unconsciously, react negatively; for example, feeling left out, using the fact of the individual sessions as a weapon ('see — you really are the one with the problem'), or seeing the therapist as being more interested in or aligned with the partner having the individual sessions. The therapist should err on the side of caution in deciding whether to see just one or both partners individually.
- The individual sessions should focus on the partner who is present, not on the absent partner. Often it is helpful to have a ground rule about not talking about the behaviour or motivations of the absent partner:

Jane is not here, so we cannot really know *why* she might have said that. The important question, anyway, is how *you* made sense of what she said — what happened to you when you heard her say that?

- If there have been more than a few individual sessions with one partner, it is important to have a session (or two) with the other partner before resuming conjoint sessions: this enables the therapist to re-engage with that partner, and balances up the therapeutic alliance before going back into conjoint sessions.

David and Leanne (referred to in Chapter 5), had started to make some significant progress with communicating in a more open and intimate manner during the first six conjoint sessions. It became clear, however, that David (a highly successful professional, with a PhD) struggled with a great deal of self-doubt. This led him to be anxious and thus somewhat rigid and problem-solving when Leanne wanted to talk more intimately. They frequently got stuck in circular arguments in the sessions as David tried to explain himself in a way that had far more to do with his anxiety than with Leanne. It was agreed that he would have four individual sessions to explore his self-doubt in more detail — the therapist feared that doing this in the conjoint sessions would focus too much on David's difficulties in Leanne's presence, increasing his anxiety. In the second individual session it became clear that in David's family, when he was young there had been a great deal of emphasis on 'what others might think'. The therapist was able to reframe an adolescent incident that David had always felt particularly ashamed about — to his visible relief. The four individual sessions were enough to remove the roadblock, allowing David to start to share in the conjoint sessions much more openly about his vulnerability. In the next conjoint session the therapist began by asking Leanne how it had been for her to have a break in the conjoint therapy whilst David attended sessions on his own, and then asked David if he would like to share with Leanne any thoughts coming from the individual sessions.

What do therapist and couple talk about in the conjoint session?

Once the assessment phase of the couple therapy is over, what should be the focus of the subsequent conjoint sessions? To express this question in its simplest way, what do therapist and couple talk about? This becomes a particularly pertinent question for the couple therapist when the couple look to him or her to give a lead or to set an agenda — 'you're the expert'!

The view that we are putting forward in this book is that if the relationship is to change, then there needs to be change in the way that each partner perceives and experiences the other, both consciously and unconsciously. Such a change will hopefully lead on to changes in the way that they engage with and respond to each other. The focus, therefore, is on *the space between* the two partners and on what happens within that space as the internal object world of each partner encounters both the real object of the other partner and the other partner's own internal object world (Ruszcznski, 1993).

Toby grew up in a family where his parents could not easily have fun, and where any of his spontaneous behaviour as a child was likely to be greeted with 'don't be silly'. Both his parents were people who had been traumatized by their experiences in Europe in the Second World War, and his mother, in particular, was highly critical of him. In therapy he came to recognize that his 'laziness' as a child was a form of passive/aggressive retaliation towards his mother. In his relationship with Wendy, Toby was the passive, withdrawing partner; he wanted the relationship to improve, but it seemed that he did nothing to contribute to this. Wendy complained bitterly that he could not be relied upon to take any responsibility or initiative, with practical tasks around the house, with parenting, or sexually.

One session began with Toby stretching out expansively — and somewhat seductively — on the two-seater couch in the consulting room, whilst Wendy took an armchair opposite him. The therapist began with a query addressed to them as a couple: 'where would you like to begin today?' Wendy said, somewhat acerbically, to Toby 'you're looking very relaxed today, you can start'. Toby complied, starting to give a slow and cautious report on the week since the last session, explaining rather apologetically that not much had happened between them as a couple because they had both been very busy, himself especially. As he spoke, his body language gradually changed — he sat up on the couch, looked down, and his shoulders dropped.

The therapist commented that it seemed as if Toby felt he had to give an account of himself to Wendy, and expected her to find him wanting; he wondered whether Toby experienced Wendy in his own mind much as he had experienced his mother when he was young. What followed was an important discussion, with Toby talking for the first time — cautiously and hesitantly, but directly — about his sense that whatever he 'put out' to Wendy was never enough and he always knew he would be criticized. He went on to describe how he was becoming increasingly tired of that way of being with Wendy, he did not deserve to be treated like that. As he spoke, there was the beginning of a sense of adult solidness in his voice, a sense of entitlement, that had not been noticeable before. Toby was starting to have more sense of himself as a separate person to Wendy, and to be less afraid of her. That inevitably led to his more direct and more confident expression of his anger with Wendy.

As the therapy continued, something was changing in the marital interaction between Toby and Wendy, in the transitional space (Crawley & Grant, 2001; Grant & Crawley, 2001) of their relationship. Toby began to experience himself less as a misunderstood child and more as an adult who had choices. Consequently, there was a change in the interpersonal interaction between them as Toby began to stand up for himself more actively and assertively. Kohon (1986) refers to 'the specific way in which the subject apprehends his relationship with his objects': Toby was apprehending — understanding, becoming aware of — an aspect of his relationship with Wendy that had previously been outside his conscious awareness.

How do we access this 'space between' and what happens in it? In the example just given of the therapy with Toby and Wendy, the unfolding and exploration of the way Toby unconsciously experienced an aspect of his way of relating to Wendy evolved naturally from the way they talked about what had — or had not — happened between them during the week. There was nothing particularly 'deep' or complicated about the content that they brought into the session. However, as they had a simple conversation about how their week had been, something happened in the mind of Toby to do with the way he experienced, and therefore the way he engaged with, Wendy. The therapist was able to notice Toby's apparent move into the stance of a cautious (and perhaps guilty) child as he described the week he and Wendy had experienced, and this enabled the therapist to open up that powerful but unconscious dimension of their relationship as a couple.

The answer to the question 'what do we talk about?' is surprisingly simple: we talk about *any aspect of the couple's experience of their everyday life together that they choose to talk about*, however unimportant it might initially seem to be. As the Scharff & Scharff (1991) express it,

> With or without children, long-term intimacy develops through negotiating the trivia of everyday life.
> It follows that couple therapy is conducted through discussion of these central trivia. In work with marital partners, that which has been split off, repressed, and handled by unconscious projective identification in the individual is manifest in the interaction between the partners as they review matters of daily interaction with us. It is this review that gives marital and family therapy so much access to the intimacies of shared unconscious family life.
>
> (p. 10)

. . . and how do we talk about it?

It is tempting at this point to think in terms of interventions, things the therapist does, that influence the course and outcome of the therapy. In some of what follows interventions are discussed. Far more importantly, however, we want to convey a way of thinking about the couple and their relationship, and then a way of being with the couple that flows from that thinking. It is the thinking about and the way of being with the couple that enables the therapist to apprehend, and then to bring into the awareness of the couple, unconscious aspects of their relationship — the invisible relationship — that need to be modified if the relationship is to change. It is the therapist's task to create and maintain the safe space within which new thinking about, and new experience of, each other and their relationship is possible for the partners.

Working with the 'couple state of mind'

The 'couple state of mind' is a key construct for the couple therapist. This phrase describes the capacity of a partner in a relationship to simultaneously be a participant *and* to stand outside the relationship and think about it — a capacity that in turn makes possible a more reflective and less reactive participation in the relationship (Morgan, 2001). Couples who are distressed may have never achieved a 'couple state of mind' or may have temporarily lost this capacity and feel unable to recover it without the help of a third party. In a distressed relationship, each partner feels overwhelmed by their own emotional experience and believes that the relationship will only change if the other partner changes. This, of course, is a recipe for deadlock as each tries to change the other. Each feels in some way 'attacked' by the other, and cannot contain the strong feelings associated with this. The emotional response of each partner to this sense of attack further escalates the distressing and escalating conflict or distance in the relationship. For such distressed couples, the therapist must try to provide the couple state of mind by not only 'being able to be subjectively involved with both individuals, but also, at the same time, being able to stand outside the relationship and observe the couple' (Morgan, 2001, p. 17).

The therapist needs to provide this function until the couple can themselves gain some capacity for experiencing and thinking about themselves *as a couple* as well as two separate individuals. The therapist temporarily provides from himself or herself the 'third position' for the couple, described by Britton (1989) as 'a capacity for seeing ourselves in interaction with others and for entertaining another point of view whilst retaining our own, for reflecting on ourselves whilst being ourselves' (p. 87).

This involves the therapist in trying to gain and hold an empathic awareness of the experience of each partner as an individual, even when engaging with the other partner. At the same time the therapist maintains a capacity to think in a neutral and objective way about the relationship and about the unconscious marital interaction that occurs in the space between them. It is interesting to compare this psychoanalytic concept of the couple state of mind with the phenomenologically similar description given in Bowen's family systems theory (described in Chapter 3). Bowen theory stresses the importance of the therapist maintaining a differentiated position in the presence of an emotionally volatile couple — that is, the therapist being able to think about feelings and to talk about that thinking about feelings — in the face of the partners' emotional reactiveness, which eventually enables them to become calmer and adopt a more differentiated stance in the session.

The hope in couple therapy is that eventually the partners will themselves be able to possess a couple state of mind and, even if it slips from their grasp at times of stress, to know that they will be able to regain it.

Providing holding

The ideas of holding and of containment have already been introduced as elements of psychoanalytic theory in Chapter 1. We now need to revisit these ideas, and look more specifically at how they can be helpful to the therapist working with couples.

Winnicott (1965) gives us two ideas that can be useful in illuminating the idea of the safe space in couple therapy. There is his idea of holding and the holding environment, and also his related idea of the transitional space. The experiential essence of what is meant by 'the holding environment' is captured by an image of the mother cradling an infant — an 'arms-around holding', to use an evocative term — so that a secure environment is created for the infant. The mother's role is a protective one that enables a sense of total dependence for the infant within which there can be continuity, a sense of 'going on being', for the baby. This then enables the innate process of emotional development, including one-to-one relating, to occur. Later, holding and the provision of a holding environment creates a safe psychological space *between* parent and child, a transitional space, in which the young child can bring together, play with, and start to integrate all the different bits of his or her experience — what Ogden describes as 'an unobtrusive state of "coming together in one place" that has both a psychological and physical dimension' (Ogden, 2004). Picture a parent patiently and attentively listening to the bitty, fragmented speech of an excited or distressed 3-year-old child, providing the space in which all the bits of the child's experience can all be got out, played with, and gradually brought together in a more integrated way. Winnicott's understanding of the holding environment is primarily focused on the infant's physical and sensual experience of the mother and the environment she provides as she adapts to the infant's needs, an environment in which there can be continuity of the infant's experience over time.

Translating this to couple therapy, the therapeutic 'frame' of planned and regular times for meeting, along with the empathic, non-judgemental style of the therapist, and the therapist's efforts to listen and to understand, hopefully gives rise to a growing sense of empathic attunement of therapist with each of the partners. This, along with the therapist's capacity to maintain a couple state of mind, leads to a sense of the therapy providing a place where each partner and their relationship will be held securely. Then there is a space in which the bits of experience — however frightening, angry, destructive, or erotic — can be safely put out, sorted through, and gradually integrated. In this transitional space, the experience of self, of partner, and of self-with-partner can be explored and responded to without an overwhelming fear of retaliation; empathic listening of each to the other — therapist to each partner; and then, hopefully, gradually, partner to partner — becomes a possibility (Crawley & Grant, 2001; Grant & Crawley, 2001).

Working with containment and projective identification, and providing containment

The psychoanalytic concept of containment, or the container/contained, is often linked with Winnicott's idea of holding and the holding environment; indeed, they are often spoken of as if they were the same phenomena described in other words. There is, however, a difference. Winnicott's concept of holding is primarily sensual, focusing on the infant's experience of the mother's physical presence and the environment she provides as she adapts to the infant's needs. By contrast, Bion's concept of container/contained is essentially about thinking, focusing on a more active process of unconscious communication between mother and infant as the mother receives, processes, and returns the infant's projections (Ogden, 2004; Symington & Symington, 1996).

In containment the image is of the mother (the container) in a state of reverie as she receives the infant's experience (the contained), which the infant is not yet able to think about or put into words — fractiousness, rage, fear, despair, or joy, contentment, excitement — taking the experience in, making sense of it and understanding it, and in doing so 'detoxifying' the experience and making it more manageable as she returns it to the infant. From this the infant eventually develops a capacity to think and to process their own emotional experience. In the therapeutic process, the therapist's presence — non-reactive, attentive, receptive — is similar to the mother's state of reverie. The therapist receives, 'takes in' and understands, and gives back the client's projected experience in a more manageable form — that is, non-judgementally, empathically, and perhaps interpreted.

Containment is one of the important psychological functions provided by the healthy couple relationship; that is, the capacity of the relationship to act as a container within which the partners are able to express their own experience and to receive and process each other's experience. This may mean receiving at times the other's despair, anger, sadness, depression, or their joy, pride, excitement, or desire; thinking about it; and giving it back in a way that enables the other to now experience themselves as heard and understood, and perhaps to think about their experience differently. For couples where such containment is not possible, escalating emotional distress will often ensue. For distressed couples, the therapist needs to create the possibility of containment — that is, to receive projected emotions or affects, not to be frightened or overwhelmed by them, and to give them back in a way that can be heard, received, and eventually talked about by the couple — thus gradually enabling the partners to be able to perform this function for each other.

In the early stages of the couple therapy, this work of containment is likely to be predominantly 'internal' work for the therapist. They will seek, through their countertransference experience, to become aware within their own subjective experience of some of the projective processes occurring in the therapy space, will struggle to hold that experience and not react to it, and then will attempt to find less 'toxic' ways of giving it back to the couple by talking about it in a more reflective and non-judgemental way. The therapist's capacity (described in Chapter 6) for 'negative capability', for being able to be content to stay in a state of confusion and of 'not knowing', without having to reach anxiously for an explanation or solution in order to make themselves feel more secure, is an important part of this process of creating a sense of containment.

In considering the process of containment, we must also revisit the process of projective identification (Catherall, 1992), where an attribute or experience of the self that cannot be owned by the person — either because it is 'bad' or unacceptable, or because it is 'good' and too precious for the person to safely keep within themselves — is split off, projected into the other, and 'found' there. The other person may identify with and express the projected quality; or the first person may unconsciously induce in the second person the expression of the projected qualities. This process, of course, is unconscious, quite outside the awareness of the two people involved, although there will often be a sense of something 'not quite fitting' or not being right. For example, a person might find it difficult to own the angry and destructive part of themselves; they find a partner who is comfortable with expressing anger, or whom they 'make angry', and who thus expresses that attribute for them. If the first partner experiences their anger as 'bad' and denies it is part of them, then they are likely to criticize or attack it in the second partner when the second partner expresses it. Or a person may value but be afraid to own an attribute — for example, their intelligence, their artistic ability, or their eroticism — but they find a partner into whom they can project that overvalued part of themselves for safe keeping, whilst they deny possession of that attribute. The expression of the attribute by the second partner will then be enjoyed vicariously by the first partner, or may come to be the focus of envy and even hatred.

Object relations theory sees projective identification as having its origins in early infancy, and as being a normal aspect of the functioning of the personality, something we all engage in at some level. Projective identification is '. . . retained as a mental process of unconscious communication that functions along a continuum from defence to mature empathy' (Scharff & Bagnini, 2002). In a couple relationship a reciprocal process of projective identification provides the basis for the unconscious bonding between the two partners, as each finds and enjoys repressed or denied aspects of the self in the other in a process that leads to a greater sense of integration of self for both (Scharff & Bagnini, 2002). However, where there is a defensive, rather than mature, need for projective identification, distress in the relationship may well result.

The couple therapist needs to develop a sensitivity to the patterns of projective identification operating in a couple's relationship. To bring this unconscious process to the couple's awareness the therapist finds opportunities for appropriately naming and talking about the projections, thus enabling the partners to 'take back' into themselves their more defensive projections.

Recognizing the process of projective identification is not always easy, and requires that the therapist possess an ability to use their own sense of self in the therapy. This requires a capacity for 'negative capability', of being able to 'not know', and an awareness of their own countertransference experience. Acknowledging that the concept of projective identification is difficult to describe and may sometimes sound a bit mysterious, Scharff & Bagnini (2002) state as follows:

> We can become aware of it from its effects upon us as therapists (and ideally also in our domestic life as spouses). It is usually experienced as a feeling that is alien or unexplainable, perhaps a feeling of excitement or numbness. It can be a sudden idea, a fantasy, a sense of in-touchness, or a fear (such as a fear of going mad).
>
> (p. 62)

Mike and Sally, who presented for help with constant, bitter fights following Mike's involvement in an affair over a prolonged period, provide an example of some of the processes we have been describing.

> In the initial sessions of the therapy, Sally was incandescent with rage and hatred, whilst Mike was provocatively laconic and reasonable — there was none of his anger in sight. The therapist had to struggle with his own countertransference experience — one of anger towards Sally, for being so unreasonably and continuously angry and attacking; and of aggressiveness towards Mike for being so provocatively dismissive of Sally and the therapist. This aggressiveness felt different to the therapist than just anger, more a sense of wanting to *get* Mike to attack him, to punish him. Over a number of sessions, the therapist was able to receive Sally's rage and hatred, and tried not to be frightened or overwhelmed by it. In response, Sally seemed gradually to have less need to flood Mike with her rage. A theme of her attacks had been that she could not possibly trust Mike again; however, she was able to start to own the terrifying fear of abandonment that had fuelled her rage. As Sally's anger became more contained, the passive/aggressive aspect of Mike's behaviour became more visible. It seemed that perhaps Mike was actually the angrier of the two partners, but had never been able to let himself experience the extent of his (to him, very frightening) anger. This made sense in the light of his early life experience of abandonment. He had projected his anger into Sally, and through the affair recruited Sally into acting it out for

him. Mike could then criticize Sally, pointing out how unacceptable and unreasonable her rages were — in effect, attacking his own unacceptable anger that Sally was now expressing.

Working with transference and countertransference

An unconscious dimension, 'the invisible marriage' (Shaddock, 1998), operates in each couple's relationship. This invisible marriage is inevitably present in the therapeutic system created in couple therapy, giving rise to the web of transference and countertransference relationships operating between the two partners, between the individual partners and the therapist, and between the couple and the therapist (Grant & Crawley, 2002). The therapist will inevitably feel the pull of this web, and will also contribute to it. To understand more fully some of what is experienced by the partners in a relationship, as well as what is experienced by the couple therapist during the therapy session, we must give attention to the phenomena of transference and countertransference.

An important distinction, especially in couple therapy, is that between the contextual transference and the focused transference (Scharff & Scharff, 1991). The Scharff & Scharff illustrate this distinction by describing the difference between the mother providing the *context* for the relationship with her baby — making sure the baby is cared for, clean, warm, comfortable — and the mother's *focused engagement* with her baby through eye contact and attunement to the baby's experience. The former they call the 'arms-around holding' relationship, the latter they call 'centred holding'. From this they move to describe the two forms of transference. First, a patient in therapy relates to the therapist in terms of their previous experience of 'arms-around holding' in relationships; their hopes and/or fears about being 'held' contribute to the *contextual* transference to the therapeutic situation. Second, a patient brings into the relationship with the therapist expectations and fantasies derived from specific experiences of focused engagement in earlier relationships; the range of such experiences — the hopes, fears, excitements, and rejections — involved in those earlier relationships gives rise to the *focused* transference to the therapist.

These two forms of transference are both present and important in conjoint couple therapy. The partners bring to the therapy the pattern of focused transferences to each other that have developed over time. They also bring a shared contextual transference 'built around their shared hopes and fears about the therapist's capacity to provide therapeutic holding by shoring up their deficient ability to provide holding for themselves' (Scharff & Scharff, 1991, pp. 65—66). Whilst individual partners may develop a focused transference to the therapist in conjoint couple therapy, it is the shared contextual transference that is more obvious and to which the couple therapist will give more attention.

The other side of the transference coin is the experience generated in the therapist by the focused and contextual transference of the couple — in other words, the therapist's countertransference to the couple's transferences. The therapist's capacity for 'negative capability', 'a state to sink into, best achieved by not doing too much and allowing understanding to come from inside our experience' (Scharff & Scharff, 1991, p. 109), allows the therapist to discern what is being generated within them whilst with the couple. Referring to the contextual countertransference, Scharff & Scharff (1991) describe how the 'internal parental couple' of the therapist is significant in reading the unconscious processes in the distressed couple:

> We each have many versions of couples inside us, just as we have many versions of families inside. These versions express angry couples, loving couples, and idealised and feared couples. At different points in the transference, different aspects of the internal couple constellation and the corresponding affects will be sensed by therapists in the countertransference. The most immediate clue to the kind of relationship being stirred up inside is the set of emotions that come into play. This clue leads to the couple's contextual transference to the therapist and its resonance with their shared projective identifications or transferences to each other.
>
> (Scharff & Scharff, 1991, p. 73)

As the therapist learns to recognize their own countertransference experience in the conjoint session, this becomes one of the most important resources that the therapist has available in seeking to understand something of the unconscious processes, the invisible marriage, of the couple (Solomon & Siegel, 1997). For example, the therapist may become aware of a sense of 'walking on eggshells' with a particular couple, and experience hesitation in asking questions or making responses that normally would come easily. The therapist is, in their countertransference, picking up the unconscious anxiety experienced by the couple, who are experiencing the therapy as a highly dangerous place. Recognizing that this is happening, and finding a way to talk about the anxiety the couple might be feeling, may lead to the couple's anxiety becoming more conscious and manageable, and the therapy becoming less threatening.

> Glenys and Martin were a professional couple in their late thirties, who had one daughter aged 4. They presented for therapy because of the unpleasant disagreements they were having, which were increasing in frequency; they feared that if they did not do something about it, they might end up divorcing. In the assessment process they described lives that focused on their professional careers, with long hours of work for both of them. There seemed little sense of relaxation or of enjoyment in anything they described: even parenting their daughter was spoken of in terms of the difficulties of the roster for getting her to and from childcare. They reported sexual activity in their relationship had been almost non-existent for some considerable time.
>
> Prior to the second conjoint session with Glenys and Martin, the therapist found himself thinking about them, and was aware of not looking forward to the session. The feeling was one of emptiness and bleakness. The session started with Glenys and Martin wanting to discuss a practical difficulty that they thought might contribute to their arguments. The therapist looked for an opportunity to comment that whilst listening to them he was aware of a sense of bleakness and loneliness about their relationship — it was as if they were each sitting on opposite sides of the room, and had given up hope of being able to meet each other in the middle. They both acknowledged that this resonated with their experience — and as the session went on they began to explore, very slowly and tentatively, that they would like to be able to be different with each other.

Conclusion

This chapter has described some aspects of the therapeutic process in couple therapy. Two aspects of the overall structure of the therapy were considered: (i) the question of whether stages could be discerned in couple therapy; and (ii) the question of whether the therapy should involve both partners in conjoint sessions. The chapter then focused on some of the therapeutic processes in conjoint couple therapy, with a central focus on the therapist's 'way of being' with the couple, rather than on a range of techniques. This led to a consideration of 'what should be talked about' and 'how should it be talked about'. The last part of the chapter addressed issues such as the 'couple state of mind', holding, containment, projective identification, and transference and countertransference.

8

THE DYNAMICS OF PRESENTING PROBLEMS

There are a number of specific presenting issues in couples work where an understanding of the underlying dynamics is important. This chapter outlines four common scenarios, and provides some points for the therapist to consider in assessing the couple and in structuring the therapy. These four scenarios are as follows:

1. an indication of the possibility of domestic violence;
2. an extramarital affair;
3. a re-married couple with stepchildren;
4. a polarized position for the two partners about whether or not they want to stay together.

Domestic violence

Over the past 20—25 years awareness of the frequency and serious-ness of domestic violence has grown enormously. Previously coun-sellors and psychotherapists, along with many others, were all too often guilty of minimizing the significance of domestic violence, regarding it as a 'private' matter or blaming the recipient of the violence (Smith, 1989). The pendulum then swung the other way as domestic violence began to be taken more seriously, and it was often stated or implied that counselling — especially conjoint couples counselling — was not an appropriate response to domestic vio-lence; rather, it should be viewed as a matter for the police, and facilitating immediate separation of the partners was the only responsible course of action (Sherman, 1992; Sherman & Berk, 1983, 1984a,b). The field is now hopefully, moving into a more balanced position, where it is realized that domestic violence is indeed a serious and potentially life-threatening situation, but where careful assessment is important and a response is needed that is tailored to the particular situation.

The couple therapist will, inevitably, be faced with new cases where domestic violence is apparent or where the therapist suspects that there may be a history of domestic violence. As indicated in Chapter 5 when discussing assessment, this is one situation where it is vital that the therapist meets individually with each partner as part of the assessment process. In such cases the safety of the recipient of the violence and of children in the family is paramount; however, for the risks to be properly assessed, the therapist needs to obtain information that enables some key questions to be answered. This information must be obtained in a way that does not trigger further violence or increase the danger to the recipient of the violence: both naïve optimism about what can be achieved through conjoint therapy and a knee-jerk reaction that refuses therapy can be profoundly unhelpful. To manage this delicate process, the couple therapist first needs to understand something of the nature of violence in the couple relationship.

Understanding domestic violence

The use of physical violence in a relationship is never justified and is morally and socially unacceptable. For one person to physically assault another is an offence in most legal jurisdictions, especially if the assault results in an injury. The fact that the two parties to the violence are also spouses or partners, or that the assault occurs in the privacy of their home, should not constitute an extenuating circumstance. At the same time, it also has to be acknowledged that violence that occurs between partners is not a unitary phenomenon; there are different forms of violence, and different constellations of factors that lie behind such violence. The couple therapist therefore faces the difficult task of ensuring that violence is not condoned and taking appropriate steps to ensure the physical safety of the recipient of the violence, but at the same time still seeking to understand the violent behaviour in the context of the particular relationship and the particular life stories of the two individuals concerned.

The spectrum of violence in couple relationships

Therapists are presented with a wide range of stories about violence in relationships. Consider these three scenarios:

1. In response to a question about physical violence, a couple report that on two or three occasions over the course of their 20-year relationship one of them has reacted violently during a heated argument — has pushed or slapped the other, or has thrown something. The other partner is clearly not afraid of the partner who committed the violent acts, and talks about what happened quite comfortably: they say that they have stated firmly that such behaviour is unacceptable, and it has not occurred again. In such a situation, it is almost equally likely to be the female as the male partner who committed the act of violence (Fergusson, Horwood, & Ridder, 2005; Holtzworth-Munroe, 2005). Quite often there would have been a story of reciprocal violence — one partner has acted violently, and the other has in turn responded with violence.

2. A couple both agree that there has been no physical violence in their relationship, but there is a frequently occurring pattern where one partner becomes exceptionally angry and the other partner is intimidated by their anger. For the intimidated partner, life in the relationship revolves around keeping the peace, trying to 'mind read' the angry partner so as to avoid another frightening flare-up of anger. This sense of intimidation is apparent in the way one partner relates to the other in the telling of the story. It could be either partner who does the intimidating, but is far more likely to be the male partner, who is also physically more powerful.

3. A couple present with a story of one partner getting into a rage and physically attacking the other, quite possibly so severely as to result in significant physical injury. This has happened more than once, and the frequency of the attacks might well have become greater over time; a consequence is that the partner who is the recipient of the violence lives in a state of constant fear and intimidation.

There have been a number of attempts to develop distinguishing criteria between different types of domestic violence and between different types of perpetrators of domestic violence (Dutton, 1995, 1998; Holtzworth-Munroe & Stuart, 1994; Jacobson & Addis, 1993; Johnson & Ferraro, 2000). A helpful discussion by Johnson (1995; 2005) suggests one way of distinguishing between these scenarios, based on an analysis of the pattern of control in the relationship. Reviewing the sociological research literature on domestic violence in North America, Johnson (1995) argues that two different pictures of domestic violence are found. One picture, which tends to come from research using a qualitative methodology and with a feminist orientation, results from research with domestic violence populations — that is, the subjects of the research are people living in women's refuges or involved in domestic violence treatment programmes. The other picture results from quantitative research, which draws its data from surveys of large-scale and randomly selected samples of the general population.

These two pictures of domestic violence, argues Johnson, are strikingly different in what they indicate about the frequency, patterns, and dynamics of domestic violence. It has been assumed that these differences are the result of diversity in research methodology, creating vigorous debates about the research methods. Johnson, however, suggests an alternative explanation: both pictures are correct, he argues, because each gives an account of a *different* phenomenon. There are, in effect, two different forms of couple violence that occur: 'situational violence' (initially termed 'common couple violence' by Johnson) and 'intimate terrorism' (initially termed 'patriarchal terrorism'). Both these patterns have been placed under the broad rubric of 'domestic violence', yet they differ markedly in terms of gender symmetry/asymmetry (whether the violence is likely to be committed by the male or the female), how frequently the violence occurs in the relationship, the presence or absence of a pattern of escalation (the 'cycle of violence'), and the extent to which reciprocal violence occurs.

Situational couple violence occurs where '. . . conflict occasionally gets "out of hand", leading usually to "minor" forms of violence, and more rarely escalating into serious, sometimes even life-threatening, forms of violence' (Johnson, 1995, p. 285). Situational couple violence is a phenomenon rooted in the dynamics and interactional patterns of the particular couple's relationship, and is a by-product of their inability to manage the expression of strong negative affect in their relationship.

Intimate terrorism, on the other hand, is described as '. . . a product of patriarchal traditions of men's right to control "their" women, is a form of terroristic control of wives by their husbands that involves the systematic use of not only violence, but economic subordination, threats, isolation, and other control tactics' (Johnson, 1995, p. 284). Intimate terrorism is thus a phenomenon based on a systematic exercise of power by one partner to intimidate and control the other.

Johnson's identification of these two types of violence, whilst open to debate, nonetheless serves a useful function for the couple therapist. It provides a stimulus and a road map for exploring the nature of the violence, rather than just reacting to the presence of violence.

Every relationship is unique and Johnson's typology is a useful resource in exploring the details of violence in a particular couple relationship. Looking back at the three scenarios given above, it is clear that the first scenario fits the 'situational couple violence' category, and the other two have features of the 'intimate terrorism' category. It is also clear that interventions appropriate for the first scenario would not be appropriate for the other two, and particularly not for the third scenario.

In addition to intimate terrorism and situational couple violence, Johnson & Ferraro (2000) also identify two other types of violence that occur. These are 'violent resistance', primarily perpetuated by women against a controlling and/or violent partner, and 'mutual couple violence', where both partners are controlling and violent — 'two intimate terrorists battling for control' (p. 950). More recently, Holtzworth-Munroe, Clements, & Farris (2005) have referred to

a growing consensus in the field that there are differing types of violence that may have differing causes. Specifically, lower levels of violence (e.g., minor violence, often engaged in by both partners, and usually studied in community and young samples) are beginning to be viewed *as having dyadic causes*, whereas more severe violence (severe and/or frequent violence, often studied in clinical or criminal samples, and often found to be more male perpetrated) is increasingly viewed as being *caused by individual characteristics of the violent male partner.*

(p. 1123, italics added)

The dynamic of violent behaviour in intimate relationships

The question of why some relationships are violent has naturally attracted a great deal of interest. Although domestic violence, particularly of the intimate terrorism type, may be a feature of a patriarchal social system, this does not explain why some people resort to violence whilst others, faced with similar circumstances, do not. One strand of enquiry has concerned the characteristics of the perpetrator of the violence (Dutton, 1998; Holtzworth-Munroe & Meehan, 2004; Holtzworth-Munroe & Stuart, 1994; Holtzworth-Munroe, Stuart, & Hutchinson, 1997). We need to understand why certain men use violence, while others who are equally disappointed or angry use other means such as negotiation or withdrawal (Siann, 1985). There are some useful pointers both from psychodynamic theory and from empirical studies in social psychology.

Dutton (1998) argues that

A triad of early factors — witnessing abuse, being shamed by a parent, and being insecurely attached through unpredictable parental emotional availability — constitutes the basis of the adult abusive personality. These three components produce an emergent reaction: intimate dysphoria [i.e. unease or discomfort in intimate situations], blamed on the partner, and a tendency to ruminate culminating in explosive abuse.

(1998, p. viii, parentheses added)

As discussed in Chapter 2, self psychology has suggested that rage is essentially defensive, rather than destructive. Thus, for example, an experience of overwhelming shame may lead to a defensive reaction of rage (Kaufman, 1989; Kohut, 1977); this rage can be understood as an attempt to hold together a sense of self that is experienced as fragmenting or disintegrating under the weight of shame, and as an attempt to ward off further experience of shame. It is like the drowning person, who in desperation thrashes around and lashes out and 'attacks' someone who is trying to rescue them.

Retzinger (1991), a social psychologist, provides another view of this from laboratory studies of marital interaction. She argues that in protracted conflict there is a hidden cycle of unacknowledged or disowned shame. This leads to the defensive affect of anger/rage, then to conflict, and thence to increased social separation, with the likely development of a cycle of shame, rage, and withdrawal in the relationship. She concludes as follows:

Many dysfunctional communication patterns have their roots in shame and shame-rage; the amount of unacknowledged shame during a quarrel seems to reveal the level of destructiveness. It must be remembered that shame itself is not destructive. Shame is a normal and necessary part of human organisation. The way it is managed is the source of concern.

(p. 199)

Whilst understanding some of the factors that lie beneath violence in a relationship does not condone or excuse the violence, it does point to a major challenge facing the therapist: how can the situation be managed so that safety is ensured for the recipient of the violence and for any children involved, whilst at the same time ensuring that the underlying issues are addressed in an effective manner. Whilst violent behaviour towards a partner is abhorrent, perpetrators of domestic violence are also usually individuals in profound need of help: the challenge is to find a way to engage them so that they can receive that help.

When faced with a situation of 'intimate terrorism', the couple therapist needs to keep in mind that the couple relationship itself often has its own unique dynamic. Goldner et al. (1990) and her colleagues reported on clinical research on relationships where violence was entrenched. The team worked with couples with long-term problems involving domestic violence, where there were repeated reconciliations after a violent episode. Their study suggested that both the women and the men in their caseload were socialized into a view of what it meant to be a man or woman that made abuse in a relationship more likely. The women had been taught that they were responsible for their male partner's emotional well-being, leading to a pattern of accommodation in the face of abuse and violence. The men had been shamed into denying vulnerable aspects of themselves, often by an abusive relationship with their father; this left them craving for intimacy, which they found frightening when it looked like occurring. Most importantly, this research described the hidden, shamed, love and attachment the couple felt for each other — a bond which the research team termed 'the alliance' — that endured despite repeated violent episodes: 'since it is a bond termed by others as shameful, sick, and regressive, it remains a secret, hidden from the world' (p. 359). This understanding of 'the alliance' has considerable significance for the therapist working with such a couple:

> to react only to the violent "face" of the behaviour without viewing its other face, the face of atonement and redemption, is to deny the power of the bond that fully possesses the couple. . . . *The strength of this bond has the potential to defeat the most persuasive shelter or anti-battering program: the more outside forces try to separate the couple, the more the bond binds them together. . . .* (T)hus, unless this powerful bond is given its due, the relationship will not be visible in all its aspects, and the couple's bond will become a secret coalition against all outsiders, including the therapists.
>
> (p. 359, italics added)

Thus, they argue, an important task in therapy with couples where there is a history of repeated serious violence is to bring the experience of this powerful bond into the discourse of the therapy:

For these reasons, early in our work with these couples, we listen for any positive descriptions of their relationship, and we encourage those commentaries as part of our therapeutic conversation. Making space for this kind of dialogue takes away the binding power of the secret.

(p. 359)

Responding to domestic violence

The principle we would want to advocate is that when domestic violence is, or might be, part of what a couple bring to therapy, the therapist must proceed cautiously and not begin to work with the couple in conjoint therapy unless there are grounds for being confident that it is safe to do so. In many instances, and especially in situations of 'intimate terrorism', there will be considerable work to be done with the individual partners first (Jenkins, 2007). It is important to 'err on the side of caution' and suggest other strategies of help, including individual therapy. If, however, careful examination suggests that the violence falls *clearly* into the 'situational violence' category, conjoint therapy may well be an appropriate interventive strategy. The task then becomes one of exploring the interaction around the violent incident, and the ways in which the two partners handle conflict. Of particular importance will be a focus on the affective experience that led to the inappropriate expression of anger — fear of abandonment, shame, and so on — and helping the partner concerned to own, contain, and express such feelings without needing to resort to violence. One practical step the therapist can take to ensure that they have not been overly optimistic in assessing the couple's relationship is to schedule a further individual session with each partner after one or two initial conjoint sessions; this will enable the initial assessment that this was not a situation involving intimidation to be re-examined in the light of additional knowledge and a more established therapeutic relationship.

Affairs

Another situation that can create a dilemma for the couple therapist is the couple who present because of the disclosure of an affair. The sense of betrayal experienced by one partner, and the guilt and shame often experienced by the other partner (or, conversely, their denial of the significance of what has happened), frequently results in a volatile first session with the couple. It is important that the therapist is 'able and willing to think carefully about the ramifications for all parties likely to be significantly affected, and not to simplify this into a choice between supporting the prior or the latter relationship or to favour one marital status or gender over another' (Cornwell, 2007).

The future of the relationship after the disclosure of an affair is, most importantly, something only the couple themselves can decide. However, if the relationship is to survive, and if there is to be growth precipitated by the crisis, rather than a return to the status quo, it is important to shift the focus *to* the couple's relationship and *away from* a preoccupation with the affair. Yet this must be accomplished without denying or trivializing the anger and deep hurt caused by the affair, and the often very serious wound to the betrayed partner's self-worth.

It is helpful to think in terms of three sequential tasks when a couple present because of an affair: managing the crisis of the affair, moving from blame to a focus on the couple's relationship, and working on issues that emerge in the relationship.

Managing the crisis of the affair

This will involve providing a sense of containment for the strong affect and reactivity that is often involved. With the betrayed partner this will involve engaging with their anger and with their hurt and grief beneath the anger over the loss of trust in the relationship, and also over the impact of the affair on their sense of self-worth. With the partner who has had the affair, it will involve working with issues such as their guilt and shame, or perhaps their inability to understand and empathize with their partner's distress ('Why is he/she making so much of it, I was drunk and it was only a one-night stand', or 'it was just sex, I never really cared about him/her'). It may also mean acknowledging their grief over the ending of the relationship with their lover, a grief that they cannot let their partner know about.

Moving from blame and guilt to a focus on the couple's relationship

The second task involves moving to a point where the affair is seen as a point of potential growth for the relationship, and as perhaps reflecting existing (although sometimes unacknowledged or unrecognized) difficulties in the relationship. As the Scharff & Scharff comment, the therapist will often find that 'the discovery of an affair crystallizes dissatisfaction due to marital discord that has been at a low boil for years' (Scharff & Scharff, 1991). The challenge for the therapist in this second step is around timing — if the therapist moves too quickly, they run the risk of being seen as unsympathetic to the betrayed partner or as condoning the affair and minimizing its importance. Nonetheless, it is often helpful for the therapist to hold in mind the fact that affairs can, when the couple are ready, be reframed in a positive way.

Working on issues that emerge in the relationship

Once the focus has moved to the relationship, the work from this point on is essentially the same as therapy with any other relationship difficulty — with the proviso that often the wound caused by the betrayal will need to be revisited and 'worked through' over a period of time whilst trust and emotional intimacy is gradually rebuilt. Moreover, the meaning of the affair, both for the relationship and for each of the partners, will need to be explored: for example, does the affair represent some split-off or denied part of the self of the partner who had the affair that they could not (and perhaps still cannot) allow into the marriage. Scharff & Scharff (1991) provide a helpful discussion of viewing affairs in this way.

A number of writers have suggested typologies of affairs, trying to divide affairs into a number of sub-types with common underlying dynamics, and drawing upon a range of psychodynamic and systemic theoretical viewpoints; these are summarized by Weeks, Gambescia, & Jenkins (2003). Such typologies are useful as a source of preliminary hypotheses, providing a stimulus for exploration of the underlying dynamics of the affair and of the relationship, but it is important not to use the typology as a diagnostic tool to categorize couples and force their unique story into fitting a pattern. As Weeks et al. (2003) caution, the category can become the defining characteristic 'often truncating the process of gaining a deeper understanding'. Thus the Scharff & Scharff' caution that 'there are as many causes of affairs as there are individuals having them' (1991, p. 221).

Brown (2001) offers one of the more useful typology of affairs that assists the couple therapist to understand some of the underlying dynamics. A brief summary of the five categories of affairs she identifies is as follows:

1. *Intimacy avoidance affairs*
   Just when there might seem to be a possibility of increased intimacy in the relationship, an affair gives the couple something to fight about and thus maintain distance, and this can go on

indefinitely — 'how could you possibly expect me to trust you again after what you did?' and/or 'you're always looking for an opportunity to bring up that one time that I slipped up'. These affairs often happen relatively early in the relationship.

2. *Conflict avoidance affairs*
   In these affairs the main dynamic is an attempt to get a response from the partner to dissatisfactions with the relationship. Such couples typically cannot tolerate conflict, and thus raising issues directly with each other is too threatening. The affair is like a 'hand grenade' tossed into the relationship, it cannot be ignored — or can it? Again, conflict avoidance affairs can occur quite early in a relationship.

3. *Sexual addiction affairs*
   Some individuals need the excitement of a new relationship or the challenge of a new conquest in order to maintain a sense of aliveness and being lovable. They often move from affair to affair. When the excitement starts to wear off in a relationship, these individuals experience an intolerable sense of being empty, alone, perhaps emotionally dead, in their internal world. Brown describes the theme of the person who has numerous affairs as 'fill me up, I'm running on empty' — an evocative phrase that conveys the underlying dynamics; it also perhaps counteracts the sometimes rather medical meaning that is given to the term 'addiction', with an associated minimization or denial of responsibility by the person who sees themselves as 'addicted'. Pittman (1989) uses the term 'philandering' to describe these affairs. Often there is a degree of unconscious collusion from the partner, who ignores the warning signs of another affair as long as possible, or is endlessly forgiving of the infidelities; but eventually something happens that cannot be ignored, or they start to change and have a little more sense of their own entitlement. Frequently there is remorse from the person having the affair, but this can be deceptive since it is often part of the cycle. Breaking this cycle requires the 'addicted' individual to address some of their own personality difficulties through therapy, and this is likely to be a lengthy process. Therapy for the other partner is also indicated to assist them with issues around self-worth, entitlement, and the maintenance of clear boundaries in the relationship so that they are not pulled back into a caretaking role towards the unfaithful partner.

4. *Split self affairs*
   Here the relationship, rather than the individual, feels empty. These are usually affairs that occur later in a relationship, often

after children have become independent and the couple are faced with — but do not succeed in — building a new level of intimacy in their relationship. Sometimes there is an awareness on the part of the partner having the affair that the relationship is empty, sometimes they themselves are surprised when they suddenly find themselves involved in an emotionally intense affair. The prognosis for such affairs is often not good, despite the desire of the unfaithful partner to maintain the marriage — sometimes there is very limited emotional connection left in the relationship.

5. *Exit affairs*

A typical scenario here is where one partner wants to end the relationship but is unable to acknowledge this to their partner (and sometimes not even to themselves), often because they cannot face the anticipated hurt and anger of their partner. In having an affair, they consciously or unconsciously hope it will be discovered and result in the end of the relationship. For the partner involved in the affair, participating in counselling is often not really about wanting to save the relationship, but more about hoping that the counsellor will look after the other partner whilst they leave. Brown's description of such affairs is 'help me make it out the door'.

In addition to these possible categories, we must also take into account that some relationships or marriages are based on an assumption — or even on an explicit understanding — that sexual and/or emotional fulfilment can only be found elsewhere than with the partner. Such situations include where there is an illness or physical disability that makes sexual activity difficult or impossible, or where the partners feel an obligation to stay together (for example, for religious reasons or to provide a home for their children) despite having no sexual or emotional interest in each other. Sometimes such arrangements can lead to unanticipated difficulties, resulting in therapy being sought.

Whatever the underlying dynamics of the affair, there are three important questions that often arise for the couple therapist who is working with a couple where there has been an affair.

Must the affair have ended before couple therapy can be undertaken?

Should the therapist work with the couple knowing that one partner is secretly involved in an affair or is continuing an affair that they have told the other partner they have ended? Our response to this question would be 'no' in almost all situations. It is not really feasible to work with a couple to clarify whether or not they want to continue their relationship, let alone to improve their relationship and to rebuild trust and intimacy, if one of the partners is still actively but secretly involved emotionally and/or sexually with a third party. It is also questionable from an ethical perspective for the therapist to conduct conjoint couple therapy knowing this to be the situation. That is one of the reasons why, as described in Chapter 5, when an affair is the part of the presenting problem it is essential for the therapist to take the 'long route' to assessment and to have an individual session with each partner as part of the assessment process. The individual session with the partner who has had the affair then gives an opportunity to explore what that partner means when they say that the affair has ended.

In the first conjoint interview Simon assured his wife Annette and the therapist that his affair of several months with a younger female colleague had ended. Annette expressed doubt about this; she was not sure how she could trust Simon when he had been deceiving her for several months. In a subsequent individual session, when pressed for details by the therapist, Simon explained that the affair was ended in the sense that he and his lover had agreed not to engage in a sexual relationship again, or go out socially. However, he admitted that he still had long and intimate conversations with her several times a week — as he saw it, she was emotionally needy, had been going through a hard time, and needed his support, which he had a duty to provide to her. He had not told his wife about this continuing contact because he knew she would be unreasonable about it; and in any event this was now just a friendship with a colleague since there was no longer any sexual activity involved, and it was up to him who he had as a friend. He was surprised and angry when the therapist questioned whether the affair had really ended. He refused to either talk about the situation honestly with his wife or end contact with his lover, and couple therapy did not proceed.

Another variation on this situation is where the affair is ended in the sense that the partner and lover have agreed not to have contact for a period of time, but there is an understanding between them — explicit or implicit — that the lover is 'waiting in the wings' and is available to resume the relationship if the attempts to reconcile the marriage are unsuccessful. Again, the commitment of the unfaithful partner to the marriage has to be addressed and clarified, and the affair clearly ended, if serious couple therapy is to be embarked upon.

Having stated the principle, however, it is important to acknowledge that there will be occasions when implementing it will be difficult and may require flexibility to be exercised by the therapist. This is a situation where supervision or consultation with an experienced colleague is particularly important to clarify the issues involved and to try to identify any countertransference issues the therapist is not aware of.

What is the therapist to do about secrets?

This leads inevitably to the second question: what should the therapist do if they find out in the individual assessment session with the partner who has been unfaithful that the affair is continuing, despite the assurances given to the other partner that it is ended. Our view is that the therapist then has to make it clear that conjoint couple therapy is not possible in such circumstances, and to work with the individual partner to clarify what they really want to do. Sometimes — and this is often underestimated in importance — the unfaithful partner genuinely wants to reconcile with their partner and end the affair, but the degree of emotional involvement in the affair makes separation from the affair very painful. There is grieving for the lost relationship with the lover that needs to take place, and this is usually a hidden grief because the betrayed spouse understandably cannot tolerate hearing about it — for them the lover is a 'bad' person, the relationship should never have happened, and there is nothing to grieve for.

For the therapist to say that conjoint couple therapy cannot proceed because he or she has learnt that the affair has not ended can, of course, create a dilemma or a crisis for the partner who is still involved in the affair. Weeks et al. (2003) provide a helpful discussion of this issue, where they label their approach as 'accountability with discretion'. In essence, when a secret is disclosed to the therapist, they make it clear that the partner holding the secret will need to make a decision whether to continue the affair or to end it and work on the primary relationship. However, they suggest that the therapist may also agree to maintain confidentiality about the continuing affair for a specified period of time whilst they work with the partner to accept responsibility for their behaviour by making a choice and taking the appropriate action. Ultimately, however, the therapist may need to point out — honestly, compassionately, but firmly — that the dilemma the partner faces is not of therapist's making. In doing this, the therapist is highlighting the contradictions embedded in the position the person holding the secret is taking — that they want to work towards a better relationship with their partner, but are not prepared to be honest whilst doing so. The therapist is creating a 'crucible' (Schnarch, 1991) for that partner — and this may in the long run be the most helpful thing to do for them.

A similar dilemma occurs, of course, when a couple come for help with a difficulty about a problem that has nothing to do with an affair, but in the assessment process one partner discloses an ongoing or recent affair. We take the same position: it is not appropriate to — for example — work with a couple on improving intimacy or communication and at the same time know that one partner is investing their emotional energy in another relationship. Again, the partner who is involved in the affair needs to be faced with the dilemma they are in — they will need to end the affair if they want to work on improving their relationship through engaging in conjoint therapy — but a time frame may need to be negotiated with that partner within which the therapist will work with them on reaching a resolution to their dilemma.

In discussing in Chapter 5 a framework for assessment that involves an individual meeting with each partner, we stressed the importance of clarifying the ground rules about confidentiality at the start of the individual session. If this procedure is followed, the therapist is not then in a position to break the confidentiality of the individual session and tell the other partner about a continuing affair that is disclosed. But neither can the therapist be required to collude in deception of one partner by the other. Occasionally, however much the therapist tries to help the partner with a secret come to a decision about the affair, the therapy comes to a premature end, which can be painful for the couple and unpleasant for the therapist. Contrary to the concerns of beginning couple therapists, this seems to happen only very occasionally. However, we need to keep in mind that affairs — involving, as they inevitably do, betrayal — will by their nature generate strong emotions and a high degree of ambivalence: a therapist cannot seek to help couples involved in such situations and at the same time structure the process so that the 'messiness' of the affair is kept at arm's length.

What about the question 'how can I ever trust him/her again?'

This is a very obvious and reasonable question. It also one that, so long as it is needing to be asked, gives an indication that the betrayed partner has not yet been able to work though the narcissistic wound (Livingston, 2001; Shaddock, 2000) of the betrayal. An answer we often give is to point out that trust is not a commodity that can be given: rather, it is a by-product of the quality of the relationship between two people. Only as the two partners start to experience a new degree of openness and intimacy with each other will the question of betrayal recede into the background and trust start to rebuild. The partner who has been betrayed needs to be helped to reach a point where they feel secure enough in themselves to be able to state clearly that if the relationship is to continue, then any further betrayal is unacceptable; and then to 'let go' and let the other partner be responsible for their own future behaviour and its consequences.

The re-married couple with stepchildren

One of the major changes that have occurred in family structure over recent generations has been the increased rate of marital breakdown, and the consequent increased rate of re-marriage or re-partnering for one or both partners. When two adults form a new relationship, and bring children from the previous relationships of one or both of them into their new relationship, they create a context for their couple relationship that is particularly complex. An extensive literature, both clinical and research, has developed about the complexities of stepfamilies (Bray, 1995; Gorrell-Barnes, 2004; Hetherington & Kelly, 2002; Visher & Visher, 1988), and it is important for the couple therapist to be familiar with this research.

Here we want to briefly sketch out some of the issues that need to be considered when a couple who are in a stepfamily situation seek help. Part of the stress for such couples will often be tension between step-parent and stepchild, and in some instances the stepchild may appear to be serving as a scapegoat for the difficulties in the couple's relationship. Our experience is that there are three questions that the couple therapist needs to address in the re-married family system with stepchildren.

1. *To what extent is there 'unfinished business' from the previous relationships of one or both partners that needs to be resolved?*
   This will involve exploring how the previous relationship came to end, the meaning that was attached to that ending, and the extent to which associated emotional issues have been worked through. These questions need to be explored with each partner, and — if judged appropriate — with their child or children, and initially

will often need to be addressed in one or more individual sessions without the new partner present. Often the necessary mourning for the relationship, and the healing of the wound to the sense of self-worth of the parent and the children, will have progressed; but where this process has become stuck, or has been denied or avoided, therapeutic work is often needed so that the past relationships can be disentangled from the present ones. Occasionally, a carefully planned session involving the partner, the ex-partner, and their children is indicated.

2. *What was the process for forming the new relationship?*
   There are two issues to be explored here. First, for the two new partners, what was the experience and dominant motivation that led them to decide to live together or marry? Was this a consequence of their feelings for each other, or was it, at least in part, to avoid being alone and/or to provide a two-parent family for their children? In other words, the therapist needs to 'deconstruct' the experience and process of decision-making about the formation of the new relationship. Sometimes this has been consciously and thoughtfully worked through by the new partners as a couple; but in other instances assumptions have been made and conclusions drawn that play an important role in subsequent difficulties. The second issue needing to be explored is the process by which the children of each partner were involved in the move to form a stepfamily system. Was this explained to the children in an age-appropriate manner and worked through over a period of time, with the children's feelings allowed expression and taken seriously? Or were the children told about a *fait accompli*, perhaps with little notice of the change that was to occur?

3. *How have roles and relationships in the new stepfamily system been negotiated?*
   After the first two questions have been explored, and a context for the current couple and family system established, this third question can be addressed. There are obvious new roles and relationships between step-parent and stepchild(ren): were these negotiated, with time for transition, or were they assumed and imposed? Issues here include matters of inclusion and exclusion (there can be a marked sense of loss for a child who has to give up a valued role in a single-parent family), discipline, and affection (even expectations about names can be highly significant). For adolescents there are perhaps issues about what constitutes appropriate sexual boundaries with a step-parent of the opposite gender. For the children there may be issues about a perceived (or feared)

change in their relationship with their biological parent, and there may be complicated roles, relationships, and boundaries (for adolescents, sometimes including sexual boundaries) to establish with new step-siblings. Issues of loyalty to the non-resident biological parent may be evoked.

Working with couples in step-family systems presents some common traps for unwary players. Often, since such couples frequently present with step-parent/stepchild difficulties, therapists attempt to move into the here-and-now task of negotiating roles and relationships between adults and children/stepchildren before exploring, and, if necessary, working through, issues to do with the historical context of the step-family's formation.

The polarized couple

A pattern whereby one partner pursues for emotional closeness and responsiveness whilst the other distances has long been recognized in the couple relationship (Guerin et al., 1996; Kerr & Bowen, 1988; Titelman, 2003). An extreme form of this is the couple who present with polarized positions about the continuation of the relationship. In a polarized relationship one partner is wanting — and often desperate for — the relationship to continue, whilst the other partner is unsure what they want or is actively talking of ending the relationship. Sometimes the polarization is clear from the start, at other times it only becomes clear as the therapist attempts to move into couple therapy and the ambivalence of one partner about the relationship becomes apparent. A dynamic of pursuer/distancer (Johnson, 2004) is at the core of such relationships, with one partner pushing for commitment and the other partner backing further away the more they feel pressured to commit.

The couple therapist will encounter the polarized couple from time to time, although relatively little appears to have been written about this pattern: an exception is a useful collection of essays edited by Crosby (1989). In such situations, the therapist is faced with a dilemma: how do they remain neutral, given that whatever they do that is acceptable to one partner runs the risk of antagonizing the other? This is a situation where the pull into triangulation, into taking one side or the other in the dispute, is particularly strong (Broderick, 1983; Guerin et al., 1996). To explore the underlying difficulties in the relationship is often seen as a betrayal by the pursuing partner — 'I thought it was your job to save marriages, not encourage divorce!' On the other hand, to explore any positive aspects of the relationship runs the risk of being heard by the ambivalent partner as evidence that they are going to be talked into staying in the relationship. The danger for the therapist in getting caught up in the struggle between the two partners can be a very real one with such couples: how, then, is a therapeutic alliance to be formed with them as a couple?

The essential task with polarized couples can be conceptualized as a process of interrupting the pattern of 'pursuer and pursued' long enough for the partners to reflect on their situation and make a more considered decision. Each partner is typically preoccupied with the other partner's position and unable to reflect on their own position or on the relationship. A key element of the therapy becomes trying to contain the anxiety and help each partner to be more in touch with whatever is driving the anxiety — that may be a fear of abandonment for the pursuing partner, and/or a fear of engulfment for the distancing partner. The relationship may have reached a point where separation is inevitable; or it may be a relationship which is still very much 'alive', but where the couple are caught in an intense and ongoing struggle about separateness and togetherness (Klever, 1998), or are acting out an unconscious aspect of the dynamic of their relationship.

The following protocol for responding to a couple presenting with a polarized relationship is adapted from a paper entitled 'What's the Rush: a negotiated slowdown' by Russell & Drees (1989). It provides a way for the therapist to redefine both the purpose of the therapy and their role as therapist, so that they can remain neutral to the outcome in a way that is more likely to be acceptable to both partners, whilst also setting up the conditions within which they can try to create a safe space — or, at least, a safer space — for the underlying issues to begin to be explored.

- *Initial agreement*
  The therapist negotiates an agreement with the couple for a specific number of sessions — six sessions is usually a realistic target — with the goal of understanding as fully as possible the reason for the situation the couple are in, and exploring the options available to them before any final decision is reached. It often helps to point out that separation is a major decision, especially if the couple have children, and it therefore makes good sense to take time to ensure that the best possible decision is being made. The therapist will need to stress their neutrality to the

outcome — only the two partners themselves can decide whether or not to stay together — and also to assure the partners that they are willing to work with them to implement whatever decision they eventually make.

- *An individual session with each partner*
  The therapist tries to assist the anxious partner, the pursuer, to own their ambivalence about the relationship, to acknowledge that it is not perfect. It is also important to help the pursuer to start to explore what lies beneath their desperate anxiety about the relationship ending — for example, a fear of abandonment, a sense that they could not cope on their own, or perhaps a fear of the shame involved if they separate or divorce. Hopefully the therapist can begin a process of providing a sense of holding and containment that makes the anxiety able to be thought about instead of being acted out by pursuing the other partner. With the ambivalent partner, the therapist tries to explore the reality of the relationship — not only the dissatisfactions or disappointments, but also the positive aspects of the relationship and of the other partner. It is important in the individual session to try to ascertain whether they are actually ambivalent about the relationship or 'post-ambivalent' — that is, have they actually moved beyond ambivalence to being clear that they do not want to continue in the relationship under any circumstances, but have been unable to tell the other partner this directly.

- *Conjoint sessions*
  In the remainder of the agreed number of conjoint sessions, the therapist aims at helping each partner to talk about and to reflect on their experience of the relationship, and on the part each plays in the difficulties. Some shared exploration of the family of origin of each partner in the conjoint sessions is often helpful in enabling both partners to look more objectively at what they each bring into the relationship. Particular attention is given to opportunities for helping each partner to become a little more differentiated in their position about the relationship: that is, opportunities for clarifying and owning their own experience, and for being clear about and owning what each wants, rather than accommodating to the other or projecting their concerns onto the other.

- *Review and decision*
  After the agreed number of sessions, the situation is reviewed and a decision made about future directions. It is important that the therapist remains neutral to the eventual decision of the partners, including keeping to the agreement to review options after a

specific number of sessions. By this stage the partners may now see issues that they would like to work on, with a view to reconciling and staying together. Or, one or both partners may be clear that separation is the route they wish to follow.

Conclusion

A premise that underlies much of what has been said in earlier chapters is that the couple therapist needs to understand the functioning of both individuals and individuals-in-relationship, and the dynamics of relationship systems. This chapter has described four situations that can arise in couple therapy: domestic violence, affairs, re-married couple with stepchildren, and the polarization by partners of views about the future of their relationship. Some guidelines for working with these issues were presented, both in terms of the issues involved for individual partners and in terms of the dynamics of the relationship system. These guidelines will hopefully enable the therapist to provide the holding and the containment that allow therapy to proceed. In doing this, we have also indicated how in two situations — domestic violence and extramarital affairs — conjoint therapy may sometimes not be an appropriate way to try to offer help.

Epilogue: Surviving as Couple Therapist

In couple therapy the therapist is required to be able to engage with both of the individual partners at an emotional depth that is often comparable with individual therapy, but without being pulled into an alliance with one partner against the other. At the same time the couple therapist is required to think about the patterns and dynamics of the couple relationship as a whole, and about the complex triadic therapeutic system. This makes couple therapy particularly demanding as a modality of therapeutic practice, and so we conclude by looking at some issues that are important for the couple therapist in looking after their own professional well-being. The issues we look at are the research evidence for the effectiveness of couple therapy, ethical considerations particular to the practice of couple therapy, and supervision and personal therapy for the couple therapist.

Research and couple therapy

The practice of any form of psychotherapy can be discouraging at times, with the therapist left holding the unbearable affect of their clients — deep hurt, anger, sadness, or shame — and also needing to face limitations in their ability to help particular clients. The possibility of discouragement for the couple therapist is perhaps greater than for therapists working in other modes of therapy, given the high level of investment many clients have in their couple relationship, the complexity of the therapeutic process, and the depth of the distress often experienced when issues cannot be resolved. It may at first glance seem strange to include research in a chapter about survival as a couple therapist, but one practical antidote to discouragement as a couple therapist is familiarity with the evidence for the effectiveness of couple therapy. This helps the therapist to remain resilient in the face of disappointment experienced with particular couples, and it may also help the therapist stay grounded and not become too grandiose when therapy appears to work well!

As with other forms of counselling and psychotherapy, couple therapists have experienced pressure to demonstrate that they are effective in producing positive outcomes for their clients. Advocates of therapy for couples have engaged in empirical research for several decades, with the aim of identifying effective treatments, mechanisms of change, and the relevant client, counsellor, and contextual factors associated with positive outcomes (Snyder, Catellani, & Whisman, 2006). There is now a growing body of evidence that couple therapy is effective in reducing relationship distress and that treated couples are considerably better off compared to untreated distressed couples (Baucom, Shoham, Mueser, Daiuto, & Stickle, 1998; Jacobson & Addis, 1993; Snyder et al., 2006).

Some general comments on psychotherapy research

An important distinction to make in psychotherapy outcome research is the difference between 'statistical significance' and 'clinical significance' (Kendall, Holmbeck, & Verduin, 2004). A result is deemed to be statistically significant if the improvement in functioning is calculated to be beyond what would be anticipated from chance alone — therefore it can be attributed to the intervention. Clinical significance, on the other hand, refers to whether the target problem has been significantly addressed by the therapeutic intervention; an example of this would be moving from a distressed to a non-distressed range of functioning in the couple relationship. The reason it is important to distinguish between these two types of significance is that it is possible for a result to be statistically significant without being clinically significant, and vice versa.

General findings in couple therapy research

In a comprehensive overview of research about couple therapies, Snyder et al. (2006) report that in the majority of cases, therapy for couples produces both statistically and clinically significant improvements. Shadish & Baldwin (2003) identified that 40—50% of couples show signs of clinical gains after receiving therapy, with only slightly diminished rates of improvement at later follow-up assessment. There were no significant differences in the magnitude of this positive effect across the different therapeutic orientations to couples work.

However, similar to outcome research in individual psychotherapy, the most substantially researched approach to couple therapy is the behavioural/cognitive-behavioural one. There are over 20 studies indicating that Behavioral Couple Therapy (BCT) is efficacious in reducing marital distress and improving communication (Dimidjian, Martell, & Christensen, 2002; Jacobson & Addis, 1993). Yet, in spite of these positive results, reconsideration of these studies in terms of clinical significance produces a somewhat less optimistic picture. Only about 50% of the couples had improved and only 33% of these had moved into the non-distressed range; in addition, about 33% of the improved couples underwent relapse during a 2-year follow-up study (Dimidjian et al., 2002).

Although the psychodynamic approaches described in this book are theoretically rich and were historically the first approaches to couple therapy, there is very limited empirical research. There is only one outcome study that investigates the impact of a pure psychodynamic approach (Insight-Oriented Marital Therapy, IOCT) derived from object relations and attachment theory (Snyder & Schneider, 2002; Snyder & Wills, 1989). EFCT — which derives its theoretical base from psychodynamic attachment theory, but includes experiential and humanistic interventions — has fared somewhat better with an impressive series of well-designed studies (Johnson, Hunsley, Greenberg, & Schindler, 1999).

Insight-Oriented Marital Therapy — Outcome research

Insight-Oriented Marital Therapy is a psychodynamic approach which is targeted at resolving hidden or unconscious sources of conflict in the couple relationship (Snyder & Wills, 1989). By exploring present-day destructive patterns in the relationship, therapists employing the IOCT approach seek to clarify sources of conflict by way of interpreting the underlying problems that the couple present with, then re-structuring and re-negotiating the ongoing relationship at a conscious level.

In an excellently designed randomized controlled trial (RCT), 79 distressed couples were randomly assigned to IOCT and BCT or to a wait-list control group (Snyder & Wills, 1989; Snyder, Wills, & Grady-Fletcher, 1991). At the end of therapy, couples from both treatment conditions showed marked clinical improvement in their relationship satisfaction.

Initial follow-up results from this randomized controlled trial were promising, with gains being maintained in both treatment groups 6 months after therapy (Snyder & Wills, 1989). Four years later, however, 38% of those couples receiving BCT had experienced divorce, whereas only 3% of those who received IOCT were divorced (Snyder et al., 1991). Although most of those who remained married 4 years after therapy were generally optimistic about the stability of their marriage, those who received BCT rated the likelihood of remaining married significantly more negatively. Further, it is also noteworthy that half of the divorced couples that received BCT refused to provide ratings about how helpful they found the couple therapy.

In short, it would appear from these results that the gains associated with IOCT are robust by comparison to other approaches. Although the research here represents only one study, the strength of these findings is the long-term nature of the later follow-up at 4 years.

Emotionally Focused Couple Therapy — Outcome research

EFCT is an integrative approach to couple therapy. Although EFCT does not focus on early developmental issues, it does utilize psychodynamic techniques, including identifying and accepting disowned needs; interpreting those needs in terms of underlying, less conscious affect; and the interpretation of the relationship problems in terms of this covert unexpressed affect (Snyder & Wills, 1989).

EFCT approach to couples work has been well researched, especially in terms of employing RCT methodology. In a series of meta-analyses which combined the results of four studies, Johnson et al. (1999) showed very substantial effect sizes for the therapy. This substantial effect size indicates significant clinical improvement in the relationships of these couples that means that most would have moved from distressed to non-distressed states in regard to their marriage.

A more recent meta-analysis of EFCT conducted by Elliott, Greenberg, & Lietaer (2004) corroborates these positive findings. They again found substantial effect sizes, with couples much improved post therapy.

In terms of follow-up data, there is a limited range of information available. Johnson et al. (1999) report that in 3 studies, between 38 and 50% of couples met the criteria of 'recovered' at termination, while between 70 and 73% of couples met this criteria at 2—3 months' follow-up. Using a broader range of studies for comparison, Elliott et al. (2004) report somewhat more modest termination effects.

At the very least, however, these findings show that gains from EFCT are generally maintained.

In comparison to behavioural approaches, EFCT appears to be more effective with high distress couples and at follow-up (Johnson et al., 1999). In addition, a review of five studies that compared EFCT with Insight Oriented Relational Therapy found that both approaches reported similar results for end of treatment and 12-month follow-up (Dunn & Schwebel, 1995). This provides some suggestive evidence that EFCT and insight-oriented approaches may be a better option for couples with greater distress around attachment issues.

General processes of change

Each of the major therapeutic approaches presents its own particular view about how positive changes are made. However, at present, most of these assumptions have not been thoroughly put to the test in controlled research. In some cases, theories about the process of change have been tested with mixed results. In other cases, however, therapeutic processes common to a number of therapeutic approaches have been shown to have a positive impact on relationship distress.

In EFCT research for instance, task analysis methodology has been used to identify whether the processes of change proposed by EFCT practitioners are associated with the targeted improvements (Snyder et al., 2006). In research such as this, it has been found that greater improvements are associated with deepening of experience, greater use of emotionally laden self-disclosures between partners, and shifts from hostility to affiliation strategies by couples. There is also some evidence from research of this sort showing that there are specific change processes associated with different approaches to couples work — such as the role of 'acceptance' in 'Integrated BCT' and the role of positive communication in standard BCT.

There are also a series of 'common factors' in all relational therapy that may account for improvement in couple functioning. These include the therapeutic alliance, client factors, expectancy effects and the level of intimacy in the couple. As is true in individual therapy, the therapeutic alliance is the most significant factor in predicting successful therapy outcome. Studies indicate that the therapeutic alliance in couple therapy accounts for 29% of the variance in the follow-up to treatment (Johnson & Talitman, 1997).

Within the alliance, lack of criticalness and an accepting attitude towards the couple accounted for 76% of total alliance scores (Reif, 1997). A series of papers in a recent issue of *Family Process* (Knobloch-Fedders et al., 2004; Symonds & Horvath, 2004; Garfield, 2004) both confirm the importance of the therapeutic alliance in conjoint couple therapy, and also provide further evidence of the range and complexity of the factors that influence the therapeutic alliance. We can say with some confidence, however, that the therapist's capacity to form a positive relationship with each partner, and to hold a hopeful and non-judgemental view of the relationship, is the most important factor, regardless of the interventions used.

Both IOCT and EFCT approaches to couples work show considerable merit for the purpose of addressing relationship distress and bringing about improved relationship satisfaction. Of particular note are the positive findings from medium- and long-term follow-up studies, indicating that improvements gained by couples from these approaches are generally maintained. What is also encouraging about these findings is that EFCT and IOCT both share a common orientation to the exploration of couple conflict and the deeper significance of emotional expression between the partners — these are features of relationship distress that tend to be targeted by psychodynamic practitioners.

Ethical considerations in couple therapy

Therapists are often deterred from working with couples by what they see as a potential for 'messy' ethical dilemmas to arise. Conducting a conjoint session with a couple in conflict holds considerable potential for presenting the therapist with a 'no-win' situation, where whatever they do is going to disappoint or antagonize one partner — and sometimes both partners, if the couple unite against the therapist as a common enemy! Whilst the ethical guidelines that should operate in any mode of psychotherapy are applicable to couple therapy, there are a number of issues arising from the nature of the conjoint therapy situation itself that need to be particularly kept in mind. Each of these issues is, in one way or another, related to the task of maintaining clear boundaries in the therapy. Although these issues have been discussed in earlier chapters when looking at ways of structuring the conjoint therapy process in particular presenting situations (Chapter 8), or as matters of technique (Chapter 6), they are now briefly revisited from an ethical perspective.

Recognizing that the relationship belongs to the couple

In the Introduction to this book, the point was made that the couple relationship is a social phenomenon as well as a psychological phenomenon, and in Western societies today there is a much greater diversity of form both for the couple relationship and for family relationships. Personal and social values inevitably exert a major influence on the choices that a particular couple make about the way to live out their relationship. Couple therapists themselves are not immune from holding values about relationships; indeed, as a group, couple therapists are likely to have a set of values — shaped by their professional training and experience — that will sometimes be significantly different from at least some of their clients. The couple therapist needs to be aware of their own cultural tradition and its assumptions, and to have reflected on how these will impact on their responses to the couples they work with, just as they need to be aware of their own personal 'emotional style and history' (Gould, 2007).

A particular challenge for the couple therapist is to be able to assist the couple to reflect on their relationship and question some of the assumptions it is based on, but to do so without crossing the line — a sometimes rather indistinct line — of deliberately influencing the couple towards a particular choice or decision about their relationship. A common example of where the couple therapist can inadvertently cross this line concerns a couple's decision about whether to remain together and work on their relationship or to separate. A particular therapist's value system, born of their own emotional and cultural history, may lead them consciously or otherwise to a position that gives particular emphasis to individual fulfilment, and so they subtly or directly encourage a couple experiencing long-standing difficulty in their relationship to separate. Or the therapist might personally place a high value on the importance of marriage, and discourage the couple from actively considering the possibility of separation. Other situations that can create a dilemma for the couple therapist about how directly they should influence the couple's decisions about their relationship are where there has been ongoing deception or betrayal in the relationship, emotional abuse, or issues about gender roles.

It is often helpful in such situations if the therapist can remember that as a *couple* therapist their primary role is to enable the partners to reflect on their experience of their relationship, understand something of what might lie behind their difficulties, and explore possibilities for change. To implement this role, the couple therapist may sometimes need to confront the couple about options they are not considering, but needs to do so in a way that does not take responsibility away from the couple. Whether the couple choose to change, or the specific changes they actually settle for, is ultimately their choice: literally, it is *their* relationship, not the therapist's, and that boundary must be respected. The only exception to this is when the therapist has a duty of care concerning the safety of one partner or their children, for example, with regard to domestic violence, as discussed in Chapter 8.

Sensitivity to the triangular situation and contact with individual partners

Another aspect of maintaining clear and appropriate boundaries in couple therapy concerns contact between the therapist and an individual partner. We have referred to this dilemma several times — for example, with regard to structuring the assessment phase of therapy (Chapter 5), and concerning the management of the complex issues generated around openness and secrets when there has been an affair (Chapter 8). It is often tempting for the couple therapist to want to spend more time with one partner who is particularly distressed or who seems stuck in some way. Whilst contact with one partner can be helpful, it must always occur with an awareness of possible ways in which it will be experienced by the other partner. Even when one partner seems to accept a proposal about an individual session for the other partner, such a proposal can easily be experienced — then or later — as the therapist takes sides, favouring or privileging one partner over the other. Other aspects of the triangular situation implicit in conjoint couple therapy can compound the likelihood of an unintended outcome to individual contact, for example the various permutations of gender. If a therapist meets individually with a partner of the opposite gender, what competitive fantasies might be aroused? Or if the therapist meets with the partner of the same gender, will there be fantasies about collusion? When boundaries are experienced as being violated in such a way — even though the violation is in the mind of the client, rather than involving any actual inappropriate behaviour by the therapist — trust is easily lost and very difficult to regain.

Dilemmas about contact with an individual partner can arise in numerous ways in couple therapy: a phone call from one partner after a session, wanting to clarify something that was said; a phone call requesting an individual session; a letter that is labelled as 'confidential'; or — particularly difficult to handle tactfully — when only one partner turns up for a conjoint session. Rules or guidelines are of limited help in such situations, although they can at least alert the therapist to the danger. A flexible response, based on the therapist's awareness of the dynamics of the couple's relationship and of the dynamics of the therapeutic system, is required (Shafer, 2006). Such dilemmas, whether originating in a request for individual contact or in the therapist's desire to spend time with one partner, should always be considered in terms of the transference and countertransference that might be operating. It is probably wise for the therapist to err on the side of caution in such situations, and to not be afraid to say that they want some time for reflection, explaining why they are being cautious. Central to the couple therapist's thinking when faced with such dilemmas needs to be the principle that it is the relationship that is the patient or client, not one of the partners.

Respect for the intimacy of the couple relationship

The couple therapist will need to ask a couple about emotionally intimate aspects of their relationship that are usually regarded as private to the couple; often that will include enquiring about and perhaps discussing in some detail their sexual relationship. The conjoint situation also requires the partners to talk about their experience of their relationship in the presence of the other partner, which can sometimes be a situation of great sensitivity. The couple therapist's role is therefore a very privileged one. Minuchin (1974) emphasized joining the couple's relationship system with a quality of 'mimesis', adopting where possible the couple or family's communication style and affective range, and identifying and emphasizing shared human experience. This must, however, be done in a way that conveys respect for the couple and for their relationship, rather than minimizing or trivializing their experience. Faced with the awkwardness with which some couples talk about emotionally or sexually intimate details of their relationship, it is sometimes a temptation for the therapist to try to ease the awkwardness by being blasé or flippant, or perhaps humourous — but in doing so, to unintentionally convey a disrespect for one or both partners.

The danger of inadvertently showing disrespect in this way increases when there is a gap between therapist and couple — for example, a gap of age, ethnicity, or culture, of sexual orientation, or of religious belief. A helpful safeguard is to maintain an attitude of 'respectful curiosity', of not knowing but wanting to know, especially when there is a sense of difficulty or tension in the session.

Supervision and personal therapy for the couple therapist

Most couple therapists have probably had the experience of 'losing it' in a session — of finding that their emotional reaction to the client or to the material the client is presenting has become so strong that it is unintentionally dictating how they respond to the couple or to one of the partners. Common experiences of the therapist in such situations are anger, helplessness, or perhaps anxiety and wanting to 'keep things safe'. Such situations reflect a strong countertransference response to the client, a countertransference that instead of being contained and reflected upon has evolved (or is about to evolve) into being enacted by the therapist. Bowen's (Kerr & Bowen, 1988) idea of the differentiation of self, discussed in Chapter 3, provides another way of looking at this type of situation, where the therapist can be seen to have reached the limit of their own capacity for differentiation, their capacity to think about their emotional experience and choose how they will respond. As a consequence, the therapist becomes pulled into the couple's emotional system, and begins to react emotionally instead of responding.

Due to both the complexity of the material — the interweaving of individual and systemic issues — and the emotional intensity that is often generated when a couple relationship is under threat, couple therapy presents a particular challenge to the therapist in terms of their capacity to remain differentiated, to be able to think and respond instead of reacting. Bowen (1978) himself came to the conviction that the level of differentiation of self of the therapist was a crucial element in determining the effectiveness of therapy, and consequently organized his approach to family therapy training around facilitating the differentiation of trainees. This involved an experiential process whereby trainees made an in-depth study of their own family of origin, and then engaged in a process of 'going home' (McGoldrick, 1995) to their family of origin and engaging in a process of de-triangulation. In requiring this of trainees, Bowen was asking them to undertake the same journey of differentiation of self that he himself had undertaken and described (Bowen, 1978).

We are not advocating that all couple therapists should undergo a process of work on their family of origin based on Bowen's principles. We do, however, believe that Bowen was making a fundamentally important point about the importance of the person of the therapist in couple therapy and about the use of self by the couple therapist. For the therapist to have undertaken their own psychotherapy can be of great value in couple therapy, perhaps more so than in some other modes of therapy. The aim of the personal work of the couple therapist, whatever form it takes, will primarily be to enable them to understand more of their own personal 'agenda for relationships'. What are some of the ways in which the therapist might, without initially being aware of it, be pulled into collusion with one partner over against the other partner? What are the types of experiences in relationships that resonate with the therapist's own experience, as a child in their family of origin or as an adult, making it difficult for the therapist to remain in an empathic stance with the client? What are the emotions that the therapist finds difficult to accept and to explore — sadness, anger, despair, sexual eroticism, hatred, a sense of abandonment? How does the therapist react to situations clients present that have the potential to create dilemmas about values, such as separation (or deciding not to separate, despite chronic relationship difficulties), affairs, termination of a pregnancy (or a decision not to terminate), or controlling behaviour by one partner towards the other?

Whilst personal therapy is an option the couple therapist should consider, regular supervision is not an option but, in our opinion, a necessity. From one perspective, supervision can be seen as a part of the treatment process — a means by which the couple therapist can be 'anchored' and held in the face of the powerful affective experiences of their clients. The containment of supervision enables the therapist in turn to contain the couple. From another perspective, supervision is also a vital part of the way in which the couple therapist can look after their own well-being, ensuring that they are able to keep appropriate boundaries between them and the couple. Supervision can be supplemented by a process of self-supervision, preferably using audio- or video-recording of sessions, or if that is not possible selecting some cases or sessions to write up as near verbatim as possible. A process of reviewing the recording or account of a session, and allowing time for reflecting on what was happening both in the dynamics of the couple relationship and in the therapeutic system, can provide valuable opportunities for learning, whatever the level of experience of the therapist. For some couple therapists who are unable to access appropriate supervision, such a process of self-supervision becomes especially important.

Conclusion

Couple therapy has emerged from its origins in individual and then family therapy to become a treatment modality in its own right. A recent handbook on couple therapy describes 12 separate models of couple therapy, including those from behavioural, cognitive-behavioural, psychoanalytic, strategic, integrative, and postmodern schools (Gurman & Jacobson, 2002). Although each of these models has an important contribution to make in treating distressed couples, we have focused in this book on an integration of those models which are based in the psychodynamic and systemic traditions. We have emphasized the *self in the couple relationship*, focusing on how the two individual selves of the partners, each with their own idio-syncratic developmental history, interact to form a unique couple system. We have argued that the effective couple therapist needs to be able to understand and intervene with the intrapsychic dynamics of each individual, the dynamics of the system that the couple has created, and the interpersonal relationship between the two part-ners. This is a demanding task. Consequently, the couple therapist needs to be aware of the evidence for the effectiveness of the work they undertake, thoughtful and alert to the ethical dilemmas they can be presented with, and committed to investing time and resources in their own development and support through supervi-sion and their own personal therapy.

REFERENCES

Annon, J. (1974). *The behavioural treatment of sexual problems.* Honolulu, Hl: Enabling Systems.

Aron, L. (1996). *A meeting of minds.* Hillsdale, NJ: Analytic Press.

Atwood, G., & Stolorow, R. (1984). *Structures of subjectivity.* Hillsdale, NJ: Analytic Press.

Bacal, H. (1998). Notes on optimal responsiveness in the group process. In I. Harwood (Ed.), *Self experiences in group: Intersubjective and self-psychological pathways to human understanding* (pp. 175—180). London & Philadelphia: Jessica Kingsley and Taylor & Francis.

Bader, P., & Pearson, E. (1988). *In quest of the mythical mate: A developmental approach to diagnosis and treatment in couples therapy.* New York: Brunner/Mazel.

Balfour, A. (2005). The couple, their marriage and Oedipus: Or, problems come in twos and threes. In F. Grier (Ed.), *Oedipus and the couple* (pp. 49—71). London & New York: Karnac Books.

Balint, E. (1993). Unconscious communications between husband and wife. In S. Ruszczynski (Ed.), *Psychotherapy with couples. Theory and practice at the Tavistock Institute of Marital Studies* (pp. 30—43). London: Karnac Books.

Ball, F., Cowan, P., & Cowan, C. (1995). Who's got the power? Gender differences in partners' perceptions of influence during marital problem-solving discussions. *Family Process, 34,* 303—321.

Bambling (2007). The effectiveness of relationship therapy. In E. Shaw, & J. Crawley (Eds.), *Couples therapy in Australia: Issues emerging from practice.* Melbourne: PsychOz Publications.

Bambling, M., & King, R. (2001). Therapeutic alliance and clinical practice. *Psychotherapy in Australia, 81,* 38—47.

Bartholomew, K., Henderson, A., & Dutton, D. (2001). Insecure attachment and partner abuse. In C. Clulow (Ed.), *Adult attachment and couple psychotherapy* (pp. 43—61). East Sussex: Brunner-Routledge.

Baucom, D. H., Shoham, V., Mueser, K. T., Daiuto, A. D., & Stickle, T. R. (1998). Empirically supported couple and family interventions for marital distress and adult mental health problems. *Journal of Consulting and Clinical Psychology, 66,* 53—88.

Beebe, B., & Lachman, F. (1992). The contribution of mother-infant mutual influence to the origin of self and object representations. In N. Skolnick, &

S. Warshaw (Eds.), *Relational perspectives in psychoanalysis*. Hillsdale, NJ: Analytic Press.

Bertalanffy, L. von (1969). *General systems theory: Foundations, development, applications*. New York: Braziller.

Bion, W. (1967). *Second thoughts: Selected papers on psycho-analysis*. London: Heinemann.

Bion, W. (1970). *Attention and interpretation*. London: Tavistock.

Bordin, E. S. (1979). The generalizability of the psychoanalytic concept of the working alliance. *Psychotherapy: Theory, research, and practice, 16*, 252—260.

Bowen, M. (1978). *Family therapy in clinical practice*. New York: Jason Aronson.

Bowlby, J. (1958). The nature of the child's tie to his mother. *International Journal of Psycho-Analysis, 39*, 350—373.

Bowlby, J. (1973). *Attachment and loss: Vol. 2: Separation, anxiety and anger*. New York: Basic Books.

Bowlby, J. (1988). *A secure base: Clinical applications of attachment theory*. London: Tavistock/Routledge.

Bray, J. H. (1995). Systems-oriented therapy with stepfamilies. In R. H. Mikesell, D. Lusterman, & S. McDaniel (Eds.), *Integrating family therapy: Handbook of family psychology and family systems* (pp. 125—140). Washington: American Psychological Association.

Britton, R. (1989). The missing link: Parental sexuality in the Oedipus complex. In J. Steiner (Ed.), *The oedipus complex today: Clinical implications*. London: Karnac Books.

Broderick, C. (1983). *The therapeutic triangle: A sourcebook on marital therapy*. Thousand Oaks, CA: Sage.

Brown, E. (2001). *Patterns of infidelity and their treatment* (2nd ed.). New York: Brunner-Mazel.

Brown, J. (2007a). Challenging the stereotypes of gay male and lesbian couples: A research perspective. In E. Shaw, & J. Crawley (Eds.), *Couples therapy in Australia: Issues emerging from practice*. Melbourne: PsychOz Publications.

Brown, J. (2007b). Therapy with same sex couples: Guidelines for embracing the subjugated discourse. In E. Shaw, & J. Crawley (Eds.), *Couples therapy in Australia: Issues emerging from practice*. Melbourne: PsychOz Publications.

Buirski, P., & Haglund, P. (2001). *Making sense together: The intersubjective approach to psychotherapy*. Northvale, NJ: Jason Aronson.

Carter, B., & McGoldrick, M. (Eds.) (2005). *The expanded family life cycle: An individual, family and social perspective* (3rd ed.). Boston: Allyn & Bacon.

Catherall, D. R. (1992). Working with projective identification in couples. *Family Process, 31*, 355—367.

Cecchin, G. (1987). Hypothesising, circularity and neutrality revisited: An invitation to curiosity. *Family Process, 26*, 405—413.

Cleavely, E. (1993). Interaction, defences, and transformation. In S. Ruszczynski (Ed.), *Psychotherapy with couples. Theory and practice at the Tavistock Institute of Marital Studies* (pp. 55—69). London: Karnac Books.

Clulow, C., & Mattinson, J. (1989). *Marriage inside out: Understanding problems of intimacy*. London: Penguin.

Colman, W. (1993). Marriage as a psychological container. In S. Ruszczynski (Ed.), *Psychotherapy with couples. Theory and practice at the Tavistock Institute of Marital Studies* (pp. 70—96). London: Karnac Books.

Cornwell, M. (2007). Affairs. In E. Shaw, & J. Crawley (Eds.), *Couples therapy in Australia: Issues emerging from practice*. Melbourne: PsychOz Publications.

Crawley, J. (2007). The instrument behind the lens: Holding and containment in conjoint couples therapy. In E. Shaw, & J. Crawley (Eds.), *Couples therapy in Australia: Issues emerging from practice*. Melbourne: PsychOz Publications.

Crawley, J., & Grant, J. (2001). The self in the couple relationship. Part 2. *Psychodynamic Counselling, 7*, 461—474.

Crawley, J., & Grant, J. (2005). Emotionally focused therapy for couples and attachment theory. *Australian and New Zealand Journal of Family Therapy, 26 (2)*, 82—89.

Crosby, J. F. (1989). *When one wants out and the other doesn't: Doing therapy with polarized couples*. New York: Brunner-Mazel.

Daines, B., & Perrett, A. (2000). *Psychodynamic approaches to sexual problems*. Buckingham: Open University Press.

Dallos, R., & Draper, R. (2005). *An introduction to family therapy: Systemic theory and practice* (2nd ed.). Buckingham: Open University Press.

Dell, P. F. (1982). Beyond homeostasis: Toward a concept of coherence. *Family Process, 21*, 21—41.

Dicks, H. (1967). *Marital tensions: Clinical studies towards a psychological theory of interaction*. London: Routledge & Kegan Paul.

Dimidjian, S., Martell, C. R., & Christensen, A. (2002). Integrative behavioural couple therapy. In A. S. Gurman, & N. S. Jacobson (Eds.), *Clinical handbook of couple therapy* (3rd ed.) (pp. 251—277). New York & London: Guilford Press.

Donovan, J. M. (2003). *Short-term object relations couples therapy*. New York & Hove: Brunner-Routledge.

Duck, S. (1988). *Relating to others*. Pacific Grove, CA: Brooks/Cole.

Duck, S., & Dindia, K. (2000). *Communication and personal relationships*. Chichester: Wiley.

Dunn, R., & Schwebel, A. (1995). Meta-analytic review of marital therapy outcome research. *Journal of Family Psychology, 9*, 58—68.

Dutton, D. G. (1995). *The batterer: A psychological profile*. New York: Basic Books.

Dutton, D. G. (1998). *The abusive personality: Violence and control in intimate relationships*. New York: Guilford Press.

Elliot, R., Greenberg, L. S., & Lietaer, G. (2004). Research on experiential psychotherapies. In M. J. Lambert (Ed.), *Bergin and Garfield's handbook of psychotherapy and behavior change* (5th ed.) (pp. 493—539). USA: John Wiley & Sons, Inc.

Erdman, P., & Caffery, T. (2003). *Attachment and family systems: Conceptual, empirical, and treatment relatedness.* New York: Brunner-Routledge.

Fairbairn, W. R. D. (1952). *Psychoanalytic studies of the personality.* London: Routledge & Kegan Paul.

Fairbairn, W. R. D. (1963). Synopsis of an object-relations theory of the personality. *International Journal of Psychoanalysis, 44,* 224—225.

Fergusson, D. M., Horwood, J. L., & Ridder, E. M. (2005). Partner violence and mental health outcomes in a New Zealand birth cohort. *Journal of Marriage and Family, 67 (5),* 103—119.

Ferrara, K. W. (1994). *Therapeutic ways with words.* Oxford: The University Press.

Fisher, J. V. (1999). *The uninvited guest. Emerging from narcissism towards marriage.* London: Karnac Books.

Fogarty, T. (1979). The distancer and the pursuer. *The Family, 7(1),* 11—16.

Fonagy, P. (2001). *Attachment theory and psychoanalysis.* New York: Other Press.

Fosha, D. (2000). *The transforming power of affect. A model for accelerated change.* New York: Basic Books.

Fowles, J. (1977). *Daniel Martin.* London: Cape.

Framo, J. L. (1976). Family of origin as a therapeutic resource for adults in marital and family therapy: You can and should go home again. *Family Process, 15,* 193—210.

Framo, J. L. (1992). *Family-of-Origin Therapy: An intergenerational approach.* New York: Brunner-Mazel.

Freud, S. (1905). Three essays on the theory of sexuality. *Standard Edition, 7,* 123—243. London: Hogarth Press.

Freud, S. (1909). Analysis of a phobia in a five-year-old boy (Little Hans). *Standard Edition, 10,* 1—147. London: Hogarth Press.

Garfield, R. (2004). The therapeutic alliance in couples therapy: Clinical considerations. *Family Process, 43,* 457—465.

Gendlin, E.T. (1981). *Focusing* (2nd ed.). New York: Bantam Books.

Gergen, K. J. (1994). *Realities and relationships: Soundings in social construction.* Cambridge: Harvard University Press.

Gerson, R. (1995). The family life cycle: phases, stages, and crises. In R. H. Mikesell, D. Lusterman, & S. McDaniel (Eds.), *Integrating family therapy: Handbook of family psychology and family systems.* Washington: American Psychological Association.

Goldner, V., Penn, P., Sheinberg, M., & Walker, G. (1990). Love and violence: Gender paradoxes in volatile attachments. *Family Process, 29,* 343—364.

Goldstein, E. (1997). Countertransference reactions to borderline couples. In M. Solomon, & J. Siegel (Eds.), *Countertransference in couples therapy* (pp. 72—86). New York: W.W. Norton.

Gorrell-Barnes, G. (2004). *Family therapy in changing times* (2nd ed.). Basingstoke: Palgrave.

Gottman, J. M. (1994a). *What predicts divorce?* Hillsdale, NJ: Erlbaum.

Gottman, J. M. (1994b). *Why marriages succeed or fail?* New York: Simon and Schuster.

Gottman, J. M. (1999). *The marriage clinic.* New York: W.W. Norton.

Gottman, J. M., Katz, L., & Hooven, C. (1996). *Meta-emotion.* Hillsdale, NJ: Erlbaum.

Gottman, J. M., Driver, J., & Tabares, A. (2002). Building the sound marital house: An empirically derived couple therapy. In A. Gurman, & N. Jacobson (eds.), *Clinical handbook of couple therapy* (3rd ed.). New York: Guilford Press.

Gottman, J. S. (Ed.) (2004). *The marriage clinic casebook.* New York: W.W. Norton.

Gould, D. (2007). Culture and countertransference. *Psychotherapy in Australia, 13,* 67.

Grant, J. (2000). Women managers and the gendered construction of personal relationships. *Journal of Family Issues, 21,* 963—985.

Grant, J., & Crawley, J. (2001). The self in the couple relationship. Part 1. *Psychodynamic Counselling, 7,* 445—459.

Grant, J., & Crawley, J. (2002). *Transference and projection: Mirrors to the self.* London: Open University Press.

Grant, J., & Porter, P. (1994). Women managers: The construction of gender in the workplace. *Australian and New Zealand Journal of Sociology, 30,* 149—164.

Greenberg, L., & Johnson, S. M. (1988). *Emotionally focused therapy for couples.* New York: Guilford Press.

Grier, F. (Ed.) (2005). Introduction. *Oedipus and the couple* (pp. 1—8). New York & London: Karnac Books.

Guerin, P. J., Fogarty, T. F., Fay, L. F, & Kautto, J. G. (1996). *Working with relationship triangles: The one-two-three of psychotherapy.* New York: Guilford Press.

Gurman, A. S., & Jacobson, N. S. (Eds.). (2002). *Clinical handbook of couple therapy* (3rd ed.). New York & London: Guilford Press.

Haley, J. (1963). *Strategies of Psychotherapy.* New York: Grune and Stratton.

Hammersley, M., & Atkinson, P. (1983). *Ethnography: Principles and practice.* London: Tavistock Publications.

Hardy, K. V., & Laszloffy, T. A. (2002). Couple therapy using a multicultural perspective. In A. S. Gurman, & N. S. Jacobson (Eds.), *Clinical handbook of couple therapy* (3rd ed.), pp. 569—593. New York & London: Guilford Press.

Hartman, A., & Laird, J. (1983). *Family-centered social work practice.* New York: The Free Press.

Hedges, F. (2005). *An introduction to systemic therapy with individuals.* Basingstoke: Palgrave.

Heimann, P. (1950). On counter-transference. *International Journal of Psychoanalysis, 31,* 81—84.

Hetherington, E. M., & Kelly, J. (2002). *For better or for Worse: Divorce reconsidered.* New York: W.W. Norton.

Hiebert, W. J., Gillespie, J. P., & Stahmann, R. F. (1993). *Dynamic assessment in couple therapy.* New York: Lexington Books.

Hoffman, L. (1981). *The foundations of family therapy.* New York: Basic Books.

Holmes, J. (2001). *The search for the secure base. Attachment theory and psychotherapy.* East Sussex: Brunner-Routledge.

Horvath, A. O., & Symonds, B. D. (1991). Relation between working Alliance and outcome in psychotherapy: A meta-analysis. *The Journal of Counseling Psychology, 38,* 139—149.

Holtzworth-Munroe, A. (2005). Male versus female intimate partner violence: Putting controversial findings into context. *Journal of Marriage and Family, 67,* 1120—1125.

Holtzworth-Munroe, A., & Meehan, J. C. (2004). Typologies of men who are maritally violent: Scientific and clinical implications. *Journal of Interpersonal Violence, 18,* 1369—1389.

Holtzworth-Munroe, A., & Stuart, G. (1994). Typologies of male batterers: Three subtypes and the differences among them. *Psychological Bulletin, 116,* 476—497.

Holtzworth-Munroe, A., Stuart, G. L., & Hutchinson, G. (1997). Violent versus non-violent husbands: Differences in attachment patterns, dependency and jealousy. *Journal of Family Psychology, 11,* 314—331.

Holtzworth-Munroe, A., Clements, K., & Farris, C. (2005). Working with couples who have experienced physical aggression. In M. Harway (Ed.), *Handbook of couples therapy* (pp. 289—312). Hoboken, NJ: Wiley.

Hubble, M. A., Duncan, B. L., & Miller, S. D. (Eds.) (1999). *The heart and soul of change: What works in therapy?* Washington, DC: American Psychological Association.

Jacobson, E. (1964). *The self and the object world.* New York: International Universities Press.

Jacobson, N. S., & Addis, M. E. (1993). Research on couples and couple therapy: What do we know? Where are we going? *Journal of Consulting and Clinical Psychology, 61,* 85—93.

Jacobson, N.S., & Christensen, A. (1996). *Integrative couple therapy: Promoting acceptance and change.* New York: W.W. Norton.

Jenkins, A. (1990). *Invitations to responsibility: The therapeutic engagement of men who are violent and abusive.* Adelaide: Dulwich Publications.

Jenkins, A. (2007). Becoming respectful: Approaches to relationship counselling in situations of domestic violence and abuse. In E. Shaw, & J. Crawley (Eds.), *Couples therapy in Australia: Issues emerging from practice.* Melbourne: PsychOz Publications.

Johnson, M. P. (1995). Patriarchal terrorism and common couple violence: Two forms of violence against women in U.S. families. *Journal of Marriage and the Family, 57,* 283—294.

Johnson, M. P. (2005). Apples and oranges in child custody disputes: Intimate terrorism vs. situational couple violence. *Journal of Child Custody, 2(4),* 43—52.

Johnson, M. P., & Ferraro, K. J. (2000). Research on domestic violence in the 1990s: The discovery of difference. *Journal of Marriage and the Family, 62,* 948—963.

Johnson, S. M. (1996). *The practice of emotionally focused marital therapy: creating connection.* New York: Brunner/Mazel.

Johnson, S. M. (2002). *Emotionally focused couple therapy with trauma survivors: Strengthening attachment bonds.* New York: Guilford Press.

Johnson, S. M. (2003). The revolution in couples therapy: A practitioner-scientist perspective. *Journal of Marital and Family Therapy, 29,* 365—385.

Johnson, S. M. (2004). *The practice of emotionally focused couple therapy* (2nd ed.). New York: Brunner-Routledge.

Johnson, S. M., & Talitman, E. (1997). Predictors of success in emotionally focused marital therapy. *Journal of Marital and Family Therapy, 23,* 135—152.

Johnson, S. M., & Whiffen, V. E. (2003). *Attachment processes in couple and family therapy.* New York: Guilford Press.

Johnson, S. M., Hunsley, J., Greenberg, L., & Schindler, D. (1999). Emotionally focused couples therapy: Status and challenges. *Clinical Psychology: Science and Practice, 6(1),* 67—79.

Juni, S. (1997). Conceptualizing defense mechanism from drive theory and object relations perspectives. *American Journal of Psychoanalysis, 57,* 149—166.

Kahn, M. (1989). Through a glass brightly: treating sexual intimacy as the restoration of the whole person. In O. Kantor, & B. Okun (Eds.), *Intimate environments: Sex, intimacy and gender in families.* New York: Guilford Press.

Kahn, M. (2002). *Basic Freud: psychoanalytic thought for the twenty first century.* New York: Basic Books.

Karpel, M. A. (1994). *Evaluating couples: A handbook for practitioners.* New York: W.W. Norton.

Kaufman, G. (1989). *The psychology of shame: Theory and treatment of shame-based syndromes.* London: Routledge.

Kendall, P. C., Holmbeck, G., & Verduin, T. (2004). Methodology, design, and evaluation in psychotherapy research. In M. J. Lambert (Ed.), *Bergin and Garfield's handbook of psychotherapy and behavior change* (5th ed.) (pp. 16—43). USA: John Wiley & Sons, Inc

Kernberg, O. (1987). Projection and projective identification: Developmental and clinical aspects. In J. Sandler (Ed.), *Projection, identification, projective identification* (pp. 93—115) . Madison, CT: International Universities Press.

Kernberg, O. (1995). *Love Relations: Normality and pathology.* New Haven: Yale University Press.

Kerr, M. E., & Bowen, M. (1988). *Family evaluation.* New York: W.W. Norton.

Kilian, H. (1993). On psychohistory, cultural evolution and the historical significance of self psychology — an introduction. Presented at the 16th *Annual Conference on the Psychology of the Self,* Toronto, October. Cited in Livingstone, M. S. (2001). *Vulnerable moments. Deepening the therapeutic process.* Northvale, NJ: Jason Aronson.

Klever, P. (1998). Marital fusion and differentiation. In P. Titelman (Ed.), *Clinical applications of Bowen family systems therapy* (pp. 119—145). New York: Haworth Press.

Knobloch-Fedders, L. M., Pinsof, W. M., & Mann, B. J. (2004). The formation of the therapeutic alliance in couple therapy. *Family Process, 43*, 425—442.

Kogan, S. M., & Gale, J. E. (2000). Taking a narrative turn: Social constructionism and family therapy. In A. M. Horne (Ed.), *Family counselling and therapy* (3rd ed.). Itasca: Peacock.

Kohon, G. (1986). *The British school of psychoanalysis: The independent tradition.* London: Free Association Press.

Kohut, H. (1977). *The restoration of the self.* New York: International Universities Press.

Kohut, H. (1984). *How does analysis cure?* Chicago: University of Chicago Press.

Lasch, C. (1977). *The culture of narcissism.* New York: W.W. Norton.

Livingston, M. (1995). A self psychologist in couplesland: Multi-subjective approach to transference and countertransference-like phenomena in marital relationships. *Family Process, 34*, 427—440.

Livingston, M. S. (1998). Conflict and aggression in couples therapy: A self psychological vantage point. *Family Process, 37*, 311—319.

Livingston, M. (1999). Vulnerability, tenderness, and the experience of self-object relationship: A self psychological view of deepening curative process in group psychotherapy. *International Journal of Group Psychotherapy, 49*, 1—21.

Livingston, M. (2001). *Vulnerable moments: Deepening the therapeutic process.* Northvale, NJ: Jason Aronson.

Luepnitz, D. A. (1988). *The family interpreted: Feminist theory in clinical practice.* New York: Basic Books.

Lyons, A. (1993). Husbands and wives: The mysterious choice. In S. Ruszczynski (Ed.), *Psychotherapy with couples. Theory and practice at the Tavistock Institute of Marital Studies* (pp. 44—54). London: Karnac Books.

Lyons, A., & Mattinson, J. (1993). Individuation in marriage. In S. Ruszczynski (Ed.), *Psychotherapy with couples. Theory and practice at the Tavistock Institute of Marital Studies* (pp. 104—125). London: Karnac Books.

Mahler, M. S., Pine, F., & Bergman, A. (1975). *The psychological birth of the human infant.* New York: Basic Books.

Mallinckrodt, B., Gantt, D. L., & Coble, H. M. (1995). Attachment patterns in the psychotherapy relationship: Development of the client attachment to therapist scale. *Journal of Counselling Psychology, 42*, 307—319.

Masters, W., & Johnson, V. (1970). *Human sexual inadequacy.* Boston: Little Brown.

Mattinson, J. (1988). *Work, love and marriage: The impact of unemployment.* London: Duckworth.

McCarthy, B. W. (2002). Sexuality, sexual dysfunction, and couple therapy. In A. Gurman, & N. Jacobson (Eds.), *Clinical handbook of couple therapy* (3rd ed.) (pp. 629—652). New York: Guilford Press.

McCluskey, U. (2005). *To be met as a person: The dynamics of attachment in professional encounters*. London: Karnac Books.

McGoldrick, M. (1995). *You can go home again: Reconnecting with your family*. New York: W.W. Norton.

McGoldrick, M. (Ed.) (2002). *Re-visioning family therapy: Race, culture and gender in clinical practice (Rev. ed.)*. New York: Guilford Press.

McGoldrick, M., Gerson, R., & Shellenberger, S. (1999). *Genograms: Assessment and intervention*. New York: W.W. Norton.

McGoldrick, M., Giordano, J., & Garcia-Preto, N. (Eds.) (2005). *Ethnicity and family therapy* (3rd ed.). New York: Guilford Press.

Minuchin, S. (1974). *Families and family therapy*. Cambridge, MA: Harvard University Press.

Mitchell, S.A. (2002). *Can love last? The fate of romance over time*. New York & London: W.W. Norton & Co.

Morgan, M. (2001). First contacts: The therapist's 'couple state of mind' as a factor in the containment of couples seen for consultation. In F. Grier, *Brief encounters with couples* (Ed.). London: Karnac Books.

Moultrup, D. J. (1990). *Husbands, wives and lovers: The emotional system of the extramarital affair*. New York: Guildford Press.

Muntigl, P. (2004). *Narrative counselling: Social and linguistic processes of change*. Philadelphia: John Benjamins Publishing.

Nichols, M. P., & Schwartz, R. C. (2001). *Family therapy: Concepts and methods*. Boston: Allyn & Bacon (7th ed., 2005).

Nichols, W. C. (1988). *Marital therapy: An integrative approach*. New York: Guilford Press.

Noller, P. (1984). *Nonverbal communication and marital interaction*. Oxford: Pergamon Press.

Ogden, T. H. (1982). *Projective identification and psychotherapeutic technique*. New York: Jason Aronson.

Ogden, T. H. (2004). On holding and containment, being and dreaming. *International Journal of Psychoanalysis, 85*, 1349—1364.

Person, E. S. (1989). *Love and fateful encounters: The power of romantic passion*. London: Bloomsbury.

Pittman, F. (1989). *Private lies*. New York: W.W. Norton.

Racker, H. (1968). *Transference and countertransference*. New York: International Universities Press.

Rampage, C. (2002). Working with gender in couple therapy. In A. S. Gurman, & N. S. Jacobson (Eds.), *Clinical handbook of couple therapy* (3rd ed.) (pp. 533—545). New York & London: Guilford Press.

Retzinger, S. M. (1991). *Violent Emotions: Shame and Rage in Marital Quarrels*. Sage: New York.

Rice, L. N., & Greenberg, L. (Eds.) (1984). *Patterns of change: Intensive analysis of psychotherapy process*. New York: Guilford Press.

Rief, C. (1997). Therapeutic alliance in marital therapy. *Digital Dissertations*. AAT 9812052 DAI-B 58/10 5653, April 1998.

Russell, C., & Drees, C. (1989). What's the rush? — A negotiated slowdown. In J. Crosby (Ed.), *When one wants out and the other doesn't: Doing therapy with polarised couples*. New York: Brunner/Mazel.

Ruszczynski, S. (1993). Thinking about and working with couples. In S. Ruszczynski (Ed.), *Psychotherapy with couples. Theory and practice at the Tavistock Institute of Marital Studies* (pp. 197—217). London: Karnac Books.

Sable, P. (2000). *Attachment and adult psychotherapy*. Northvale, NJ: Jason Aronson.

Satir, V. (1983). *Conjoint family therapy*. Palo Alto: Science and Behavior Books.

Satir, V. (1988). *The new peoplemaking*. Mountain View, CA: Science and Behavior Books.

Sawyer, M. (2004). Bridging psychodynamic couples therapy and Gottman method couples therapy. In J. S. Gottman (ed.), *The marriage clinic casebook* (pp. 181—196). New York: W.W. Norton.

Scharff, D. E. (1982). *The sexual relationship: An object relations view of sex and the family*. London: Routledge & Kegan Paul.

Scharff, D. E. (1989). Transference, countertransference, and technique in object relations family therapy. In J. S. Scharff (Ed.), *Foundations of object relations family therapy*. Northvale, NJ: Jason Aronson.

Scharff, D. E., & Scharff, J. S. (1991). *Object relations couple therapy*. Northvale, NJ: Jason Aronson.

Scharff, D. E., & Scharff, J. S (1998). *Object relations individual therapy*. Northvale, NJ: Jason Aronson.

Scharff, J. S., & Bagnini, C. (2002). Object relations couple therapy. In A. S. Gurman, & N. S. Jacobson (Eds.), *Clinical handbook of couple therapy* (3rd ed.) (pp. 59—85). New York: Guilford Press.

Schnarch, D. (1991). *Constructing the sexual crucible: An integration of sexual and marital therapy*. New York: W.W. Norton.

Searight, H. R. (1997). *Family-of-origin therapy and diversity*. Washington, DC: Taylor & Francis.

Searles, H. (1955). The informational value of the supervisor's emotional experience. In H. Searles (Ed.), *Collected papers on schizophrenia and related subjects*. London: Hogarth Press.

Shaddock, D. (1998). *From impasse to intimacy: How understanding unconscious needs can transform relationships*. Northvale, NJ: Jason Aronson.

Shaddock, D. (2000). *Contexts and connections. An intersubjective systems approach to couples therapy*. New York: Basic Books.

Shadish, W. R., & Baldwin, S. A. (2003). Meta-analysis of MFT interventions. *Journal of Marital and Family Therapy, 29(4)*, 547—570.

Shafer, A. (2006). Psychoanalytic Psychotherapy in the 21st Century: rigorousness, rigidity, and rigor mortis. *Australasian Journal of Psychotherapy, 25 (2)*, 34—50.

Shaver, P. R., & Hazan, C. (1988). A biased overview of the study of love. *Journal of Social and Personal Relationships, 5*, 473—501.

Sherman, L. W. (1992). *Policing domestic violence: Experiments and dilemmas.* New York: The Free Press.

Sherman, L., & Berk, R. (1983). *Police response to domestic violence: Preliminary findings.* Washington, DC: Police Foundation.

Sherman, L., & Berk, R. (1984a). The specific deterrent effects of arrest for domestic assault. *American Sociological Review, 49*, 261—272.

Sherman, L., & Berk, R. (1984b). *The Minneapolis domestic violence experiment: police foundation reports, no. 1.* Washington, DC: Police Foundation.

Siann, G. (1985). *Accounting for aggression: Perspectives on aggression and violence.* London: Allen & Unwin.

Sieburg, E. (1985). *Family communication: An integrated systems approach.* New York: Gardiner Press.

Siegel, J. P. (1992). *Repairing intimacy. An object relations approach to couple therapy.* Northvale, NJ: Jason Aronson Inc.

Silverman, D. (1997). *Discourses of counselling: HIV counselling as social interaction.* London: Sage.

Silverman, D. (2001). *Interpreting qualitative data: Methods for analysing talk, text and interaction* (2nd ed.). London: Sage.

Skynner, A. C. R. (1976). *One flesh: Separate persons; principles of family and marital psychotherapy.* London: Constable.

Smith, L. (1989). *Domestic violence: An overview of the literature.* London: HMSO.

Snyder, D. K., & Schneider, W. J. (2002). Affective reconstruction: A pluralistic developmental approach. In A. S. Gurman (Ed.) *Clinical handbook of couple therapy* (3rd ed.) (pp. 151—179). New York: Guilford Press.

Snyder, D. K., & Wills, R. M. (1989). Behavioral versus Insight-Oriented Marital Therapy: Effects on individual and interspousal functioning. *Journal of Consulting and Clinical Psychology, 57*(1), 39—46.

Snyder, D. K., Wills, R. M., & Grady-Fletcher, A. (1991). Long-term effectiveness of Behavioural versus Insight-Oriented Marital Therapy: A 4-year follow-up study. *Journal of Consulting and Clinical Psychology, 59(1),* 138—141.

Snyder, D. K., Catellani, A. M., & Whisman, M. A. (2006). Current status and future directions in couple therapy. *Annual Review of Psychology, 57,* 317—344.

Solomon, M. F. (1989). *Narcissism and intimacy: Love and marriage in an age of confusion.* New York & London: W.W. Norton & Co.

Solomon, M. F., & Siegel, J. P. (1997). *Countertransference in couples therapy.* New York: W.W. Norton.

Symonds, D., & Horvarth, A. O. (2004). Optimizing the alliance in couple therapy. *Family Process, 43,* 443—455.

Symington, J., & Symington, N. (1996). *The clinical thinking of Wilfred Bion.* London: Routledge.

Titelman, P. (Ed.) (1998). *Clinical applications of Bowen family systems theory.* New York: Haworth Press.

Visher, E. B., & Visher, J. S. (1988). *Old loyalties, new ties: Therapeutic strategies with stepfamilies*. New York: Brunner/Mazel.

Waddell, M. (2002). Inside lives: Psychoanalysis and the growth of the personality. London: Karnac Books.

Wampold, B. (2001). *The great psychotherapy debate: Models, methods and findings*. Mahwah, NJ: Lawrence Erlbaum.

Watzlawick, P., Weakland, J., & Fisch, R. (1974). *Change: Principles of problem formation and problem resolution*. New York: W.W. Norton.

Weeks, G. R., Gambescia, N., & Jenkins, R. E. (2003). *Treating infidelity: Therapeutic dilemmas and effective strategies*. New York: W.W. Norton.

Wells, S., & Taylor, G. (1987). *The complete Oxford Shakespeare: Vol. II: Comedies*. Oxford: The University Press.

Wile, D. B. (1993). *After the fight: A night in the life of a couple*. New York: Guilford Press.

White, M. (1989). *Selected papers*. Adelaide: Dulwich Centre Publications.

White, M. (1995). *Re-authoring Lives Interviews and essays*. Adelaide: Dulwich Centre Publications.

White, M., & Epston, D. (1990). *Narrative means to therapeutic ends*. New York: W.W. Norton.

Williamson, D. S. (1991). *The intimacy paradox: Personal authority in the family system*. New York: Guilford Press.

Winnicott, D. W. (1960). *The maturational processes and the facilitating environment: Studies on the theory of emotional development*. London: The Hogarth Press.

Winnicott, D. W. (1965). *Collected papers: Through paediatrics to psychoanalysis*. London: Tavistock.

Winnicott, D. W. (1971). *Playing and reality*. London: Penguin.

Wolf, E. (1988). *Treating the self: Elements of clinical self psychology*. New York: Guilford Press.

INDEX